Inaccurate Numbers, Inadequate Policies: Enhancing Data to Evaluate the Prevalence of Human Trafficking in ASEAN

JESSIE BRUNNER

EAST-WEST CENTER
COLLABORATION · EXPERTISE · LEADERSHIP

AIJI

WSDHANDACENTER
FOR HUMAN RIGHTS & INTERNATIONAL JUSTICE
Stanford University

EAST-WEST CENTER
COLLABORATION · EXPERTISE · LEADERSHIP

The East-West Center promotes better relations and understanding among the people and nations of the United States, Asia, and the Pacific through cooperative study, research, and dialogue. Established by the US Congress in 1960, the Center serves as a resource for information and analysis on critical issues of common concern, bringing people together to exchange views, build expertise, and develop policy options.

The Center's 21-acre Honolulu campus, adjacent to the University of Hawai'i at Mānoa, is located midway between Asia and the US mainland and features research, residential, and international conference facilities. The Center's Washington, DC, office focuses on preparing the United States for an era of growing Asia Pacific prominence.

EastWestCenter.org

For information or to order copies, please contact:

Publications Office
East-West Center
1601 East-West Road
Honolulu, Hawai'i 96848-1601

Tel: 808.944.7145
Fax: 808.944.7376

EWCBooks@EastWestCenter.org
EastWestCenter.org/Publications

ISBN: 978-0-86638-268-7 (print) and 978-0-86638-269-4 (electronic)

© 2015 East-West Center

Inaccurate Numbers, Inadequate Policies:
Enhancing Data to Evaluate the Prevalence of Human Trafficking in ASEAN by Jessie Brunner

Cover: About 200,000 Cambodian migrant workers fled Thailand in mid-May, 2014, amid rumors of a violent crackdown on illegal workers in that country. (Photo© George Nickels/NurPhoto/Corbis)

Table of Contents

List of Acronyms

ACMW	ASEAN Committee on the Implementation of the ASEAN Declaration on the Protection and Promotion of the Rights of Migrant Workers
ACTIP	ASEAN Convention on Trafficking in Persons
ACWC	ASEAN Commission on the Promotion and Protection of the Rights of Women and Children
AEC	ASEAN Economic Community
AICHR	ASEAN Intergovernmental Commission on Human Rights
AMS	ASEAN member states
ASEAN	Association of Southeast Asian Nations
CSEC	commercial sexual exploitation of children
CTM	Counter-Trafficking Module (IOM)
EDPS	European Data Protection Supervisor (EU)
EU	European Union
GAO	US Government Accountability Office
GSI	Global Slavery Index (WFF)
IJM	International Justice Mission
ILO	International Labor Organization
IOM	International Organization for Migration
J/TIP	US Department of State's Office to Monitor and Combat Trafficking in Persons
KPPPA	Ministry of Women's Empowerment and Child Protection (Indonesia)
MiMOSA	Migrant Management and Operational Systems Application (IOM)
MLAT	ASEAN Treaty on Mutual Legal Assistance in Criminal Matters
MSE	multiple systems estimation
NCCT	National Committee for Counter-Trafficking (Cambodia)
NGO	nongovernmental organization
SOMTC	Senior Officials Meeting on Transnational Crime (ASEAN)
THB	trafficking in human beings
TIP	trafficking in persons
TIP Report	US Department of State's annual Trafficking in Persons Report
TSS	time-space sampling
TVPA	US Trafficking Victims Protection Act
UK	United Kingdom
UN	United Nations
UN.GIFT	United Nations Global Initiative to Fight Human Trafficking
UNACT	United Nations Action for Cooperation Against Trafficking in Persons
UNIAP	United Nations Inter-Agency Project on Human Trafficking
UNODC	United Nations Office on Drugs and Crime
USAID	United States Agency for International Development
VRS	Voluntary Reporting System on Migrant Smuggling and Related Conduct (UN)
WFF	Walk Free Foundation

Executive Summary

Concern over the issue of human trafficking in Southeast Asia has grown steadily over the past several years with recent events elevating this pernicious problem to crisis levels in the public consciousness. The unearthing of mass graves in trafficking camps in both Thailand and Malaysia, the discovery of hundreds of fishermen enslaved on boats near the remote Indonesian island village of Benjina, and the steady stream of vulnerable Bangladeshi and Burmese Rohingya populations seeking refuge across the Andaman Sea have left many people speculating about the scale of the problem and struggling to find solutions.

This unsettling uncertainty arises, in part, from the lack of robust, accurate, and standardized data related to human trafficking—information critical to informing better policy to combat it. Policies and programs based on poor data will likewise be poor in their efficacy, which is why the corrective impulse should focus on collecting not just more, but better data. This data deficiency rests on the fact that those involved in human trafficking are inherently a hidden population. It is further challenged by a pervasive lack of understanding of the definition of human trafficking, corrupt practices linked to trafficking, and—whether owing to a lack of resources or an unawareness of proper research methodologies—the inability to gather and analyze such information robustly.

A desire for quantified information combined with the impossibility of accurate prevalence measures has led to largely speculative estimates of the extent of human trafficking across the globe. Though such figures are useful in drawing attention to the issue, they are often based on biased sampling methods and nebulous extrapolation techniques—not to mention they remain susceptible to politicization. Measuring trafficked populations is especially difficult because, as noted above, human trafficking is a hidden problem—meaning the total population, or sampling frame in the case of statistical analysis, is unknown—and a relatively rare phenomenon. Though the application of probability and non-probability sampling to the field of human trafficking is still nascent, there are several techniques that can be considered for estimating trafficking prevalence. Looking to methods used for measuring other hidden populations, such as the homeless, intravenous drug users, sex workers, and victims of human rights abuses, offers guidance.

Walk Free Foundation's 2014 Global Slavery Index estimated that there are nearly 36 million people in modern slavery. The figure is based on a combination of face-to-face and telephone random sample surveys, a reliance on existing studies, data reported directly from governments, in-house desk research, and communication with local experts. Critics of the index have fairly questioned its "mysterious, inconsistently applied methodology." In another estimation, the 2012 International Labor Organization (ILO) Global Report on Forced Labor relied on a capture-recapture methodology to claim there are 21 million victims of forced labor globally. In reviewing reported cases of forced labor through Internet searches and contact with nongovernmental organizations (NGOs), the ILO compared the results of two teams' investigations of secondary source material to identify overlap, and to thus extrapolate a global estimate. Though the study's limitations were acknowledged in the report, it is highly problematic that key assumptions to the statistical method were violated and, like Walk Free Foundation's Global Slavery Index, tenuous extrapolation techniques were applied.

Despite these questionable methods and the uncertain nature of the numbers they produce, few in the international anti-trafficking community seem to question the utility of global estimates in the first place. The need for a baseline upon which to measure the effectiveness of anti-trafficking policies is clear. Yet local prevalence studies based on the unique social, cultural, political, and economic circumstances of a given trafficking context seem like a preferable starting place. Also, in the process of gathering prevalence data, it is likely that local trafficking patterns will emerge, which allow for better informed, more targeted interventions. The full report highlights such studies in the Southeast Asian context, including the United Nations Sentinel Surveillance reports, which are aimed at assessing local prevalence of trafficking throughout the Greater Mekong Subregion, and International Justice Mission's (IJM) recently released follow-up study on the prevalence of commercial sexual exploitation of children (CSEC). The United Nations (UN) study of Poipet used random on-site surveys/interviews at a common border crossing for migrants returning from Thailand to Cambodia. IJM constructed a time-space sample of potential CSEC hubs throughout three cities in Cambodia and sent trained, undercover investigators to evaluate the circumstances. Obviously, any study—local or global—measuring a hidden population will be imperfect, but the more targeted the population under scrutiny, the less researchers should have to rely on assumptions and questionable extrapolation techniques.

Field study in Cambodia, Indonesia, and Thailand conducted in June 2015 revealed fundamental challenges that must be overcome before such studies will produce robust, standardized data on a regional level. First, any kind of data standardization across individual nations and the region as a whole will necessarily rely on a common conception of human trafficking and its component elements. Despite widespread adoption of the definition set forth in the Protocol to Prevent, Suppress and Punish Trafficking in Persons, Especially Women and Children (Palermo Protocol), the implementation of practices based on this understanding is more limited. Furthermore, there is little standardization of identification practices based on this definition across government entities, such as ministries, law enforcement, and the justice sector. As evaluated through policies and the allocation of resources, both financial and human, the political will to coordinate on anti-trafficking work is generally not at a level that will ensure productive collaboration and sustained, effective programming. This is further exacerbated by notable examples of corruption and collusion of government officials in trafficking rings. On a normative level, misconceptions about trafficking victims that will inevitably lead to problems in identification and data collection remain, such as the perception and treatment of victims as criminals, or the undue emphasis on sex trafficking and thus victimization of women and girls. What will arguably persist as the largest barrier to effective data collection and analysis on trafficking prevalence in Southeast Asia is the dearth of available training in social work, social science research methodologies, and statistics to apply in the anti-trafficking sphere. Insufficient training is compounded, at times, by a lack of importance placed on proper techniques, and further intensified by an unawareness of the ethical and legal standards related to the protection of personal information of trafficking survivors. Though technological tools may be available to ensure security and privacy of data, they are not often employed.

Despite these challenges, a keen awareness of the potential utility of data was consistently revealed during field interviews, as well as a desire to improve current practices. If actors across government and civil society could share information and view each other as partners combatting a common problem, they would better serve the national interest. But national coordination is just the first step. As has already been established, human trafficking continues to pose an economic, political, and social threat to the region as a whole, and efforts toward regional coordination and standardization will be needed to ensure an effective and sustainable response. ASEAN is the natural body to lead this effort and has already demonstrated a commitment to counter-trafficking under the leadership of the Senior Officials Meeting on Transnational Crime.

The launch of the ASEAN Economic Community at the end of 2015 implies greater labor and capital mobility and, with it, the potential to exacerbate the trafficking problem. With the much-anticipated November 2015 unveiling of the ASEAN Convention on Trafficking in Persons and a regional action plan that is said to include provisions for a regional trafficking database and standardized data collection, the time for action is now. The following policy recommendations are offered to ASEAN, the governments of ASEAN member states (AMS), and the international anti-trafficking community with the awareness that a transnational crime like human trafficking requires a robust, regional response, and that progress toward improved prevalence measures will require collaboration across all these entities. The following represent some of the policy recommendations from the full report.

RECOMMENDATIONS FOR ASEAN

- Owing to the often international character of human trafficking, the creation of a regional database for trafficking data is a logical and necessary step. ASEAN "ownership" of this regional database is likely the only way to secure the member state cooperation necessary for improving access to and quality of data. Careful consideration of what types of data are needed to better measure the scale and scope of the problem, along with coordination on victim identification and data collection standards, will be critical first steps.

- Robust research on trafficking prevalence will require heightened awareness and training on proper social science research methodologies, data collection techniques, and related security considerations and privacy laws.

- Any approach to combat trafficking in the region will necessitate an anti-corruption component. Despite the obvious political sensitivities in this area, research is required to develop a better understanding of the scope and manner in which corruption facilitates trafficking and impedes anti-trafficking efforts.

RECOMMENDATIONS FOR THE GOVERNMENTS OF ASEAN MEMBER STATES

- Most AMS are now party to the Palermo Protocol and have come to adopt its definition of human trafficking as their own. But more work is needed to ensure this understanding pervades the various central government institutions engaged in anti-trafficking measures, and that it permeates down to activities at the local level.

- Adequate funding must be allocated to anti-trafficking efforts on a sustainable basis to ensure their longevity and efficacy. Also, careful consideration should be made to determine which government entity, whether a ministry or task force, has the capacity and standing to effectively galvanize a diverse set of actors on the issue.

- To counteract the challenge of frequent turnover in anti-trafficking task forces and directorates throughout government, AMS not already doing so should provide better working environments. For example, more opportunities for career advancement, and incentives to stay within those tracks for longer periods of time, allow people to put their specialized knowledge and training to use. This will further encourage more robust "training of trainers," and thus enhance local capacity building.

RECOMMENDATIONS FOR THE INTERNATIONAL ANTI-TRAFFICKING COMMUNITY

- Before new global prevalence studies are undertaken, significant thought should be given to their intended purpose and design. Smaller-scale, localized prevalence studies on specific types of trafficking or designated industries should be devised. These studies should be based on the notion that smaller numbers do not automatically detract from the gravity of the issue, but invalid or unreliable estimates most certainly do.
- To prevent duplication of efforts and wasted resources, careful thought should be directed to determining what can be gleaned from existing databases and information-sharing resources before new endeavors are launched.

Inaccurate Numbers, Inadequate Policies: Enhancing Data to Evaluate the Prevalence of Human Trafficking in ASEAN

Introduction

Concern over the issue of human trafficking in Southeast Asia has grown steadily over the past several years with recent events elevating this pernicious problem to crisis levels in the public consciousness. The discovery of mass graves in trafficking camps in both Thailand and Malaysia (and ensuing charges against a senior Thai army officer for his involvement),[1] the revelation of hundreds of fishermen enslaved on boats near the remote Indonesian island village of Benjina,[2] and the steady stream of vulnerable Bangladeshi and Rohingya Muslim populations seeking refuge across the Andaman Sea[3] have left many people speculating about the scale of the problem and struggling to find solutions.

This unsettling uncertainty arises, in part, from the lack of robust, accurate, and standardized data related to human trafficking—such as numbers of trafficked persons, information on victim service provision, case information on trafficking investigations and prosecutions, and demographics of traffickers. All of this information is critical to better policies to combat trafficking, from targeting root causes to properly identifying victims to developing and evaluating the services they receive. The challenge of data collection rises from several variables, including lack of understanding of the definition of human trafficking, the black market nature of this business, and the support traffickers receive from corrupt officials. Moreover, survivors may not seek assistance or identify as victims for a number of reasons, such as fear of reprisal or stigmatization or a desire to protect implicated family members.

The simple reality is that the great majority of those involved in human trafficking are hidden. The available facts and figures reflect only those people who have been *identified* as victims or perpetrators— the tip of the iceberg. Furthermore, the international anti-trafficking community as a whole faces fundamental challenges to gathering reliable data. These challenges may arise from a lack of resources or political will at the governmental level, the inability of relevant agencies to coordinate on data sharing, or an unawareness of proper research methodologies, among other reasons. Many factors can make trafficking victims difficult to count, much less to find and assist. Because the crime of human trafficking is outlawed universally, traffickers take exhaustive measures to keep their crimes underground. Victims, in some cases deprived of personal identification documents, are often unable to move freely. Moreover, the difficulty of seeking help is potentially exacerbated by being outside of familiar social contexts and/or unable to communicate in the local language. In cases of international trafficking, many trafficking victims begin as irregular migrants, and may be unsure about their immigration status in the country of transit or destination. Fear of arrest and prosecution can make them timid to come forward. Even in familiar contexts, trauma, fear of retaliation, distrust of law enforcement, or social stigma may prevent them from accessing help.

A desire for quantified information combined with the impossibility of developing accurate prevalence measures has led to largely speculative estimates of the extent of human trafficking across the globe. Walk Free Foundation (WFF), which produces an annual Global Slavery Index, estimates there are nearly 36 million people in modern slavery today. The International Labor Organization (ILO), on the other hand, believes there are about 21 million people in forced labor situations around the world. The US State Department speculated in past years that about 600,000 to 800,000 men, women, and children are trafficked across international borders annually. Though these numbers are highly influential from an advocacy perspective, and draw much attention to the issue of human trafficking, the methods employed to produce them do not always stand up to strict scrutiny. That imprecision has led some to question what these numbers really tell us about the scale and scope of the issue.

As member states of the Association of Southeast Asian Nations (ASEAN), regional nongovernmental organizations (NGOs), and experts set out at this dire moment to comprehend the scale of the problem regionally, it is important that they carefully—and critically—evaluate existing means for understanding its breadth and depth. Moreover, the launch of the ASEAN Economic Community (AEC) slated for the end of 2015 implies greater labor and capital mobility, and with it the potential to exacerbate the trafficking problem. With the much-anticipated unveiling of the ASEAN Convention on Trafficking in Persons (ACTIP) expected in November, the time is ripe for ASEAN to consider how it can act as a regional force to ensure better data collection on human trafficking.

The aim of this report is to (1) establish a foundation of approaches for estimating hidden populations, (2) survey the field of current global and local prevalence measure methods, (3) outline normative and technical achievements and challenges that may guide the process of data collection and analysis in Southeast Asia, and (4) offer policy recommendations to advance understanding of the scale and scope of human trafficking. The report is intended both as a resource for the international anti-trafficking community to help evaluate current trafficking prevalence measures, and as a toolkit for ASEAN and those interested in the region to help set regional standards—and encourage standardization—for collecting and analyzing data on human trafficking.

SCOPE AND METHODOLOGY

The varied and complex challenges to assembling and analyzing better data on human trafficking clearly cannot be addressed in a single research study of limited time and scope. The original intention of this research was to evaluate current practices and develop suggestions for improving existing prevalence measures of human trafficking, with a focus on Southeast Asia. However, in executing the field study, it quickly became evident that more basic issues—normative, methodological, and technical—must be addressed before more accurate prevalence numbers on trafficking can be generated. There is a critical need for additional studies on improving data on numerous other trafficking elements, such as push and pull factors, demographic information on traffickers, trafficking routes, supply chains, the enabling role of corruption, and case law management. The focus of this report remains largely on assessing the sheer scale of trafficked persons.

This report is based on five months of desk research at Stanford University's WSD HANDA Center for Human Rights and International Justice, limited to English-language resources. In addition, three weeks of interviews were conducted in the field, focused on Cambodia, Indonesia, and Thailand as case studies for the region. More than 40 sources representing foreign governments, international and local NGOs, multilateral agencies, and academic experts were interviewed. Sources are cited anonymously to protect the sensitivity of information shared. The report does not purport to be comprehensive, but to provide a compilation and analysis of relevant published materials, coupled with some empirical analysis of regional trends. The initial desk research for this project revealed a lack of synthesized information on estimating hidden populations, as well as the need for an overview of current approaches in the field of human trafficking. As such, this report aims to provide a synopsis as an easy reference for those interested in strengthening data collection practices. Highlighted resources should not be taken as an endorsement of any particular organization's work. Among the vast information sources available, the resources here aim to be a representative cross-section for didactic purposes. The report also aims to provide an agenda for further studies on some of the key issues identified above.

A Note on Semantics

One of the normative challenges faced nearly universally is the tendency toward victimization of those who have been trafficked. While this report resists negative stereotypes portraying trafficked people as helpless or passive "victims," it recognizes trafficking as a crime that ultimately is about taking advantage of another person's vulnerabilities and/or limiting personal agency. Thus, the word "survivor" is generally preferable in that it represents a positive triumph over a debilitating situation. Yet too often the difference between remaining in and escaping from a trafficking situation has little to do with the individual's own choices or agency, and more to do with the coercive environment that traffickers construct and exploit. Being a "victim" who does not escape the predations of traffickers, as so many do not, does not necessarily represent personal weakness. Instead, it often arises from the circumstances, individual and social, in which the trafficked person is caught. To avoid further victimization of trafficked people, the use of the word "victim" in this report should be recognized only as a semantic limitation.

Data and Human Trafficking

A report on enhanced data collection practices would be remiss not to begin with an overview of what data is and how more data is, theoretically, beneficial. Across the field of international development, there is an increasingly emphatic push toward having more data. After all, when gathered and analyzed systematically and robustly, more data can offer seemingly infinite insights into the needs and realities of targeted populations. In addition, data aids in evaluating the effectiveness of policies and interventions aimed at serving those populations. Policies and conclusions not rooted in robust data and quality analysis are well-recognized to be limited and potentially ineffective. That said, it is problematic to view data, a nebulous concept for many, as a guarantor of quality. Policies and programs based on poor data, for example, will likely be equally poor. The focus, then, should be not only on collecting more data, but better data.

For the purposes of this report, trafficking data is understood to be any information related to human trafficking that has been collected by governments, multilateral agencies, local and international NGOs, and service providers. This could be quantitative data on the numbers of survivors served in shelters, border interdictions, or prosecutions of traffickers in domestic courts, for example. Of course, trafficking data can also be qualitative, as in the case of victim testimony, money flows, or patterns of irregular migration. However, the focus of this study is on quantitative victim prevalence data—how big the problem is on a global scale.

In the roughly two decades since re/committing to the fight against human trafficking, the international community has become increasingly aware of the need for comprehensive, reliable, standardized, and systematically collected data. Dozens of studies over the past 10 years have investigated the issue of human trafficking data collection. Frank Laczko and Marco Gramegna drew attention to this issue in 2003, acknowledging that "one of the biggest gaps in our understanding of trafficking is in the area of statistics and data collection," and that the sharing of information between countries is critical to stemming the trafficking tide.[4] While lamenting that available national statistics and global prevalence figures are generally "guesstimates," Laczko was encouraged by steady improvements to the process of estimating the scale of the trafficking problem. In 2006, the US Government Accountability Office (GAO) issued a report on the need for enhanced data and more strategic approaches to reporting and analyzing US anti-trafficking efforts overseas.[5] In that report, the GAO questioned US government estimates on trafficking prevalence, simply stating that the "accuracy of the estimates is in doubt because of methodological weaknesses, gaps in data, and numerical discrepancies."[6] Specific problems were enumerated. One issue was that a prominent estimate, developed by a single person who failed to document all of his work, proved to be non-replicable. Another issue was that the data supplied by foreign governments to the Office to Monitor and Combat Trafficking in Persons at the US Department of State (J/TIP) was problematic in terms of availability, reliability, and comparability. Dozens of other studies have identified these and other challenges, yet very few have attempted to offer succinct guidance on how to methodologically enhance the prevalence estimates. As such, reliable representations of the scale and scope of the problem remain elusive.

To navigate the "data revolution" currently underway, it is critical to have a clear idea of what precisely data is and what it can reveal, alongside a humble acknowledgment that data is not always going to be the answer to every problem, whether in the field of trafficking or elsewhere. As cautioned by Patrick Ball of Human Rights Data Analysis Group: "If you're looking at poverty or trafficking or homicide, we don't have all the data, and we're not going to....That's why these amazing [data-analysis] techniques that the industry people have are great in industry, but they don't actually generalize to our space very well."[7] That is not to say better data analysis is not a worthwhile goal; it must simply be undertaken with an awareness that problems as thorny and complex as human trafficking will require equally multifaceted solutions. A useful place to begin is with an overview of existing methods for estimating hidden populations, which will ensure a clear understanding of their limitations and a consideration of means to improve them.

Methods for Estimating Hidden Populations

By their very nature, some populations are impossible to explicitly count. They may be difficult to define or hidden, in which case identifying as a member may put a person at risk, either socially or physically. For example, one can rather easily estimate the number of children currently living in the United States, but it becomes much more challenging to measure the prevalence of children who suffer domestic abuse nationwide, much less across the globe. The case of measuring trafficked populations is especially difficult because it is both a *hidden*—meaning the total population, or sampling frame in the case of statistical analysis, is unknown—and *rare* phenomenon. Though this report will go on to establish the rather dubious nature of existing global estimates of trafficking, if the 35.8 million global figure offered by Walk Free Foundation's Global Slavery Index is accurate, that would indicate that roughly 0.5 percent of the global population is a victim of trafficking. Locating this population through simple random sample surveys, the preferred method for standard prevalence estimation, would be difficult and resource intensive in any situation. But surveying the trafficked population becomes arguably impossible given the nature of the activity, which is subject to severe legal penalties, massively profitable, often facilitated by corrupt practices, and may operate through highly organized criminal networks. Though outside the scope of this research, it is worth noting that the extrapolation of trends uncovered while analyzing data on identified survivors can be problematic. Those who escape trafficking situations and seek legal actions and/or social services may, in fact, have marked differences from the populations that remain in trafficking or decline services.

The field of statistics provides a variety of sampling and estimation techniques that can be employed to *approximate* the prevalence of hidden populations. They are summarized here with relevant examples of how they have been employed, including in the field of human trafficking, if applicable. *Because the intended audience of this report is not expected to have substantial training in statistics or social science research methodology, the use of technical terms has been minimized. That said, nontechnical readers may skip ahead to the next section on assessing prevalence measures without negatively impacting their understanding of the report in whole.*

CAPTURE-RECAPTURE

The capture-recapture, or mark and recapture, sampling method has long been used to estimate the size of a population in which the sampling frame is unknown. It was first applied to the study of wildlife populations in the 1800s—estimating the number of a given fish species in a lake, for example—and has become quite popular in epidemiological studies and in the social sciences to measure elusive populations, such as homeless people, sex workers, intravenous drug users, or HIV patients. Essentially, a preliminary sample (capture) is drawn at random from the population and marked in some way before an independent resampling of the same population is conducted, which is the recapture element. The relationship between the two samples, evaluated in terms of the overlap of those captured in both cases, allows statisticians to estimate the size of the target population. It should be noted that estimates resulting from capture-recapture methodology have relatively high variance—that is, the spread of the estimates is high—and the method's underlying assumptions can introduce biases. These assumptions include that the population is closed (the population has not changed during the study), that individuals can be easily matched in the capture and recapture phases, that individuals have the same chance of being sampled in each phase, and that the capture and recapture phases occur independently. Though employed in the ILO's global estimate of forced labor (discussed in detail in the next section), the organization recommends using this sampling method "only when other enumeration methods are not feasible."[8] This is understandable considering that human trafficking by its nature violates some of the core assumptions this methodology rests upon. In reality, the population is constantly changing and the "matching" of victims between the two survey phases is a complicated task.

MULTIPLE SYSTEMS ESTIMATION

In recent years, the use of multiple systems estimation (MSE) to evaluate the size of difficult-to-count populations has gained some traction in the field of human rights. In essence, MSE builds on capture-recapture methodology by adding additional recapture samplings. San Francisco–based Human Rights Data Analysis Group advocates its use, for example, in estimating the casualties of grave human rights violations. The group's recommendation is based on the awareness that any single casualty list (the sampling unit, in this case) will likely be incomplete due to geographical, financial, political, or other limitations. The idea is that sampling from multiple lists and analyzing the overlap allows one to estimate the "dark figure," which is the number not accounted for on documented lists of closed populations.[9] In addition to casualties of war, MSE has been used to estimate illegal wildlife smuggling and drug use. Because lists of trafficking survivors reported by service providers, anti-trafficking NGOs, and law enforcement are guaranteed to be incomplete, but likely overlapping, MSE provides a potential tool for better estimating trafficking prevalence. In fact, the method was applied last year in an exploratory analysis of the scale of human trafficking in the United Kingdom (UK). However, the study explicitly cautioned that "the findings should be treated as tentative, because the modeling includes assumptions which (though plausible) cannot be easily verified and uses data that inevitably has limitations."[10] The study analyzed data that had been collated from a broad range of sources, and ultimately gave an estimate of 10,000–13,000 potential victims of trafficking in the UK in 2013. In a recent interview, Walk Free Foundation noted that MSE might be applied to estimate prevalence in the United States in future human trafficking indices.[11]

NETWORK SAMPLING

Network sampling is commonly used to study hidden populations such as homeless people or cancer patients. Using this method, membership in a given population is determined by either directly surveying the population of potential members or by relying on official records or documents to establish membership. The latter assumes accurate, comprehensive official records, which might not be available. The technique derives its name from its method: surveyed people are asked to report the prevalence of the characteristic under study among their family, friends, professional contacts, or other networks. This technique was employed by Gallup researchers, who conducted some of the sampling research for Walk Free Foundation's recent Global Slavery Index (further elucidated in the following section). An obvious challenge lies in the issue of double counting, as researchers rarely know who is being counted in the networks of multiple interviewees.

SNOWBALL SAMPLING

Snowball sampling, a non-probability technique that is inherently less robust, expands on the idea of network sampling. Instead of asking an initial seed population to report on members of their network who belong to the group under study, snowball sampling asks those sampled to refer researchers to these connections, who are then sampled (first wave). This process is repeated a given number of times, causing the sampled population to grow exponentially. Typically, five waves is seen as sufficient to gain an accurate understanding of the given population in a limited geographic region. However, it should be cautioned that one of the downfalls of this method is that the initial sample, and each wave thereafter, is likely to recruit others with whom they share some resemblance. Also, bias is introduced at the outset. For one thing, the seed population is not randomly recruited—if they could be, they would not be considered a hidden population. For another, those people who are accessible to researchers are often not representative of the population at large. Overall, the non-random nature of this process is responsible for its downfalls being that random sampling helps eliminate biases because all individuals have an equal chance of inclusion in the survey.

Due to its non-randomness, the technique is unlikely to yield a statistically representative sample of the population at large. Although a weighting element—a statistical technique that corrects for biases—can enhance the soundness of a given study, valid conclusions cannot be drawn about the entirety of the population in question. Despite these limitations, the obvious advantage of this tactic is relatively easy access to members of a hidden population, especially in situations where identifying and/or locating them would otherwise be difficult. Hence, snowball sampling is more resource efficient, saving researchers time, money, and staff support.

This methodology was employed in Not For Sale's 2014 prevalence study on human trafficking in Silicon Valley. The study, released in October 2014, drew heavily on survey data from local service providers, as well as interviews with case managers gathered in two counties over a three-year period. The survey was designed by a team of international experts familiar with developing and implementing human trafficking monitoring systems, and it focused on collecting basic demographics, socioeconomic circumstances (past and present), and information on the trafficking experience. Participation was somewhat low, and some of those who opted not to complete the survey cited difficulty in accurately identifying clients as trafficking victims or lack of sufficient records. Not For Sale was careful to note the limitations of this sampling methodology, particularly the biases introduced by having a handpicked initial sample use their networks to select further participants. This can lead to an overrepresentation of, for example, service providers working with survivors of sexual exploitation, as opposed to those trafficked for labor. Researchers declined to estimate area prevalence, and instead attempted to describe the general nature of the trafficking situation. The methodology was also employed in Verité's recent study on forced labor in the electronics industry in Malaysia, which will be further discussed in the section on local prevalence studies.

ADAPTIVE CLUSTER SAMPLING

Adaptive cluster sampling is similar to snowball sampling, but in place of relying on the initial targeted population's network, surveyors target those in a given proximity, whether geographical or in similar demographic brackets. In the case of physical vicinity, as members of the population under study are identified, others within a predetermined geographical proximity are added to the sample. As applied to trafficking, this method could be useful if employed near border towns or high-prevalence areas, or in instances where population clustering is difficult. But like snowball sampling, careful attention must be paid to assigning proper extrapolation weights to account for the biases inherent to non-random sampling.

RESPONDENT-DRIVEN SAMPLING

Respondent-driven sampling builds on snowball sampling by applying a mathematical model (using Markov chain theory and biased network theory) that compensates for the biases introduced by its non-random nature. The technique was developed in the late 1990s as part of an HIV-prevention project and has been employed since in a number of public health studies—for example, to estimate the populations of IV drug users and sex workers. While the mathematical model is complex, the basic idea is that sufficiently long referral chains ultimately produce a sample that is independent from the seed sample. The model is further informed by analysis of the network structures created throughout the sampling waves, allowing researchers to control for bias introduced by these structures. Essentially, the various biases are quantified and used to weight the sample. If done properly, the final sample bias is believed to be trivial in samples of meaningful size.[12]

TIME-SPACE SAMPLING

Time-space sampling (TSS) is used to produce membership probability estimates of hidden populations. Venue-day-time units are constructed to represent the places, days, and times where and when this population might congregate. These units are then randomly selected for sampling, as opposed to randomly selecting a survey participant. Like similar methods, TSS has been used frequently with HIV-related projects, as well as surveying sex workers. A non-random variation of this approach was used by International Justice Mission in its study on the prevalence of commercial sexual exploitation of children in Cambodia. As opposed to targeting groups, the survey targeted specific types of establishments—karaoke bars and massage parlors, for example—for observation (as discussed further in the section on local prevalence studies).

The technique of stratification can be applied generally among these estimation techniques. Essentially, a given population is divided into various strata based on one or more characteristics—income level, education level, race, age, etc.—and independent samples are taken from each. The groupings can be oversampled or undersampled in order to get a more accurate representation of the total population. For example, a general population survey might divide the population into brackets based on income level and then sample equally among each stratum to locate the key characteristics of each subgroup. When the results are extrapolated to the population at large, however, analysts must be cognizant that each income bracket makes up a unique proportion of the total population, thus each stratum would need to be weighted accordingly. Furthermore, stratification offers researchers more keen insights into how these subpopulations may differ systematically. Applied to the field of human trafficking, researchers might consider oversampling in strata where they expect to find more cases of trafficking (such as in cities near a porous international border, rural towns identified as source hubs, or areas popular among sex tourists) in order to gain insight into the demographics of that population. They would then weight these particular strata accordingly before extrapolating out to the entire population.

Assessing Current Global Prevalence Estimates

By understanding the available research methodologies, it is possible to better comprehend how the global prevalence estimates of human trafficking that have proliferated in recent years were derived, and to better evaluate their validity. Careful examination of these estimates could be useful to ASEAN should it consider developing regional prevalence measures in the future. To reiterate, this analysis focuses on the trafficking prevalence numbers offered in the global reports discussed herein; it does not discount the wealth of information these reports offer about trafficking in various countries or about global trends.

Though global trafficking prevalence numbers—typically Walk Free Foundation's 35.8 million estimate or the International Labor Organization's forced labor estimation of 21 million—are rather ubiquitously cited as a matter of fact in NGO materials, news stories, government reports, and academic journal articles, very little academic scholarship has been devoted to critically evaluating the figures, as international human rights law expert Anne Gallagher noted in the *Guardian* last year.[13]

In April, Glenn Kessler of *Washington Post* focused his "Fact Checker" column on assessing the validity of such estimates, rating them for factual errors and/or contradictions. Kessler draws attention to the seeming incompatibilities of the US State Department citing "as many as 27 million" trafficking victims in 2013, compared to "more than 20 million" the following year. Meanwhile, WFF's Global Slavery Index estimated there were 29.8 million modern slaves in 2013, compared to 35.8 million a year later. Kessler's quote from an anonymous State Department official sums up the challenge: "The major problem we have always faced with human trafficking is finding good data....For now, this is still a guesstimate, but the best guesstimate there is."[14]

A recent piece in the *Economist* on the rising popularity and growing influence of global performance indices highlighted the fact that such rankings draw public attention and are cited by governments in an effort to change policy, despite the fact that the indices may be based on "shaky figures that are calculated differently in different countries."[15] Moreover, these indices often assume a common understanding of very subjective, vague concepts or assign numerical values to qualitative information. On a more positive note, the article highlights the effectiveness of the US Department of State's annual Trafficking in Persons Report (TIP Report). This annual compendium of governmental anti–human trafficking efforts across the globe, discussed in detail below, has effectively pressured governments to implement anti-trafficking legislation, for example. Field interviews and various media reports confirmed the extent to which Southeast Asian governments target policies and data collection to meet reporting requirements, for better or worse. The merits and drawbacks of these mechanisms for estimating trafficking prevalence are discussed in further detail here.

WALK FREE FOUNDATION'S GLOBAL SLAVERY INDEX

Australia-based Walk Free Foundation was founded in 2012 by mining magnate Andrew Forrest with the mission of ending modern slavery by "mobilizing a global activist movement, generating the highest quality research, enlisting business and raising unprecedented levels of capital to drive change in those countries and industries bearing the greatest responsibility for modern slavery today."[16] The organization has gained significant attention among the anti-trafficking community for its annual Global Slavery Index (GSI), which in its second iteration in 2014 ranked 167 countries based on the percentage of the population thought to be enslaved. (Much debate has taken place in the movement regarding use of the term "modern slavery" in place of "human trafficking" or other exploitative violations of international law, but that is an issue that requires separate treatment.) The original 2013 GSI was created to quantify the problem of human trafficking, and was allegedly spawned by advice that Bill Gates gave to Forrest: "If you can't measure it, it doesn't exist."[17]

The latest Global Slavery Index estimates that 35.8 million men, women, and children are enslaved worldwide. These results are based, in part, on face-to-face and telephone random sample surveys implemented by Gallup International as part of its worldwide poll of about 8,000 people in Brazil, Ethiopia, Indonesia, Nepal, Nigeria, Pakistan, and Russia, countries selected for regional representation and with a focus on source countries. These interviews were supplemented by WFF surveys in three additional countries—Malaysia, Qatar, and Saudi Arabia—and reliance on nine existing studies from organizations such as ILO and the US Agency for International Development (USAID). The existing studies surveyed Belarus, Bulgaria, the Democratic Republic of Congo, Haiti, Moldova, Namibia, Niger, Romania, and Ukraine. In total, 19 foundational data sources were used. Individual country prevalence was further informed by data reported directly from 38 governments (of the 167 approached), and by in-house researcher verification of data collected through desk research and interactions with local experts in 60 countries. The 2014 index represents enhancements over the original 2013 index in that it tried to paint a more robust picture of the human trafficking situation in each country (through further examination of vulnerability factors and government responses for all indexed countries), and expands the scope of random sample surveys used to supplement the desk research. For next year's index, WFF plans to conduct surveys in 19 additional countries, again in partnership with Gallup International. "Each year, we aim to rely less on extrapolation," said Policy and Research Manager Katharine Bryant in a recent interview.[18]

Final questions selected by WFF with Gallup:

1. Have you or has anyone in your immediate family ever been forced to work by an employer?
2. Have you or has anyone in your immediate family ever been forced to work by an employer to repay a debt with that employer?
3. Have you or has anyone in your immediate family ever been offered one kind of work, but then were forced to do something else and not allowed to leave?
4. Have you or has anyone in your immediate family ever been forced to marry?

"Yes" answers to any of these triggered follow-on questions.

With data from the 19 surveyed countries, Walk Free Foundation grouped all 167 countries into seven clusters based on perceived geographical, socioeconomic, and governance similarities, with each cluster containing between zero and six countries where surveys had been conducted. WFF then established what proportion of each country's population was enslaved based on weightings and comparisons to countries for which they had survey data. Needless to say, this process rests on a considerable number of assumptions, and it becomes increasingly complex and difficult to follow, even for those trained in survey methodology and extrapolation techniques. The full 79-page methodology report is available online.[19]

As mentioned, the index further ranks countries based on government response to the problem (letter rankings from D to AA, similar to a country's credit score), as well as a vulnerability dimension from 0 to 100 percent. These categories are composed of a long and fairly robust set of indicators. For example, the government response ranking tries to evaluate day-to-day practices more than simply the enactment of anti-trafficking legislation or the number of prosecutions of traffickers. The figure considers factors such as coordination and accountability mechanisms, attitudes, and societal institutions that could affect human trafficking, as well as the private sector's potential role in public procurement of goods and services that may employ forced labor. Another positive development in WFF's methodology is that it includes indicators that attempt to elucidate the gap between what a government promises or legislates versus what it delivers. The latest report integrated "negative indicators" into the ranking process, which represent actions by governments that might hinder the implementation of laws and policies that otherwise look great on paper. For example, instead of considering just the number or reach of anti-trafficking police trainings, WFF is interested in learning how many trafficking victims have been successfully identified by these trained police. Corruption is another obvious negative indicator that could impede the meaningful enactment of anti-trafficking policies.

To be fair, when developing an index of this scope, it might be expected that an entity like WFF would work behind the scenes for several years before releasing the first iteration. Instead, the group chose to work very publicly in the hopes of learning along the way. As expressed in interviews with several high-level WFF staff, there is a healthy awareness that the methodology will need to become more rigorous before year-to-year comparisons on prevalence or commentaries about overarching trends can be made.

"We are at the difficult front end of a challenging project, but for me it's about being willing to try and fail at different things so you can learn and improve," said Fiona David, executive director of global research at Walk Free Foundation and one of the lead authors of the index. "Being able to understand how big the problem is is critical—it's too important not to try."[20] David went on to emphasize how she and her colleagues appreciate constructive criticism so they can continuously improve the index. Despite the critiques, it is difficult to argue with the point that WFF has managed to draw significant attention to the issue of trafficking through the tremendous media attention given to the index and its findings. Though wary of propagating imperfect information, from an advocacy perspective, WFF has been fairly impactful.

Still, the GSI has justly attracted some ire from critics who draw attention to its complicated, and arguably messy, methodology. In the previously mentioned article in the *Guardian*, international human rights law expert Anne Gallagher candidly put forth her concerns with the index's approach, which she describes as "a mysterious, inconsistently applied methodology, a raft of unverified assumptions and multiple, critical errors of fact and logic."[21] Gallagher draws specific attention to the sometimes questionable clustering of countries. For example, China has been put in the same cluster as Japan and South Korea. In another example, South Africa's trafficking prevalence is derived from the assumption that it is 70 percent similar to Western Europe and 30 percent like its African neighbors. The overarching point Gallagher makes is that "poor information, presented as fact, contributes to poor decision making and sometimes highly damaging, unintended outcomes."[22] That said, she acknowledges that reliable, replicable data of the sort WFF aspires to gather would be immensely valuable.[23]

Like Gallagher, Andrew Guth of George Mason University—writing with a team of researchers in a 2014 issue of *Social Inclusion*—lauded the index's resource-intense goal of collecting vast amounts of primary data on trafficking, but cautioned against the danger of producing global estimates that are not easily validated. The article also expressed concern over the publicity given to the index as it means these tenuous estimates are circulated widely in the mass media, quoted by high-level policymakers and celebrities (from US Presidential hopeful and former Secretary of State Hillary Clinton to U2 front man Bono), and in academic journals. Over time, the same numbers are repeated over and over to the point that they are often offered without citation and simply given as fact. Neil Howard of the European University Institute in Florence describes such indices as a "merry-go-round of data that isn't really data….The aims may be well-meaning, but sensationalism doesn't help."[24]

Despite the criticisms, there are several elements of Walk Free Foundation's methodology and approach that are worth further consideration. First, WFF is collecting valuable data through its surveys and benefiting from the nearly unrivaled breadth of Gallup's reach. Typically this type of survey work is too resource intensive for a single entity to undertake, so it is encouraging to see significant funding and labor being devoted to this issue. Moreover, because WFF aims to publish the GSI on an annual basis, new data will be generated at regular intervals, allowing for at least loose comparability at the country level over time. As WFF expands the scope of the national surveys to more countries, yearly comparisons might be made between the extrapolated estimate for a country not initially surveyed and the estimate derived through a future survey. This will give insight into the robustness of the extrapolation techniques, which could inform improved practices in the future. Importance sampling, a useful variance reduction technique for understanding rare events, could also be considered for generating trafficking prevalence measures.

In the abstract, the motivation behind the GSI's clustering makes intuitive sense in that it is based on demographic factors thought to be related to trafficking, in addition to geography. But, as further surveys are collected, the process could perhaps be strengthened by using statistical correlation measures to test the validity of existing groupings. Another option might be using a global database like the United Nations Development Index, which could get at some of the potential root causes of trafficking—education level, income, access to social services, etc.—and use statistical analysis to stratify similar countries.

When asked broadly about the WFF methodology, a noted Stanford University–based political scientist and expert in survey methods noted that randomized surveys of this type tend to overestimate anything found in small proportions, though he recognized that this could be counterbalanced by victims' reluctance to identify or report as such. Moreover, since the survey questions use an undefined timeframe ("Have you or has anyone in your immediate family ever…?"), it seems problematic to derive a point estimate, the prevalence value at any given moment, from them. Changing circumstances—such as war, internal conflict, natural disasters, and seasonal changes—may produce ebbs and flows of varying duration in the vulnerability of targeted populations, and thus affect survey results. Suggestions to potentially augment the robustness of the surveys included randomly asking about different groupings in the surveyed person's social network—individual, family, best friends, full social network—as well as varying the timeframe (in the past one year, five years, ten years, or ever) and comparing results. In the end, "this is one of those impossible problems, so one shouldn't be overly critical," he said.

INTERNATIONAL LABOR ORGANIZATION'S GLOBAL ESTIMATE OF FORCED LABOR

The International Labor Organization (ILO) released its first global report on forced labor in 2001, calling the rising incidence of forced labor and human trafficking the "underside of globalization." It should be noted here that forced labor, as defined by the ILO's 1930 Convention Concerning Forced or Compulsory Labour, essentially encompasses all forms of human trafficking outside of organ trafficking and forced marriage or adoption. In 2001, the ILO was careful to avoid a prevalence estimate as it seemed "not possible at this stage to give an accurate estimate of the numbers affected on a global scale."[25] However, after two years of research and vast input from the internal Statistical Development and Analysis Unit, as well as academia, international and local NGOs, and governments, the follow-up report in 2005 gave a minimum global estimate of 12.3 million forced laborers. That figure was based on what was admittedly an "experimental" capture-recapture methodology. The methodology was revised and enhanced to give a 2012 estimate of 20.9 million men, women, and children being victims of forced labor globally— seemingly the most oft-cited statistic in the anti-trafficking community and media reports as of late. The ILO noted that despite similar methodology, the 2005 and 2012 estimates should not be compared for discerning trends; the latter was simply a "more robust estimate."[26]

In place of surveying people directly—as Walk Free Foundation did, in part, for its Global Slavery Index—the ILO's statistical units consisted of reported cases of forced labor. In essence, these are cases reported in a variety of secondary sources, such as the media or NGO, government, and academic reports. To be relevant, recorded incidents of forced labor had to include a given number of victims, a location, and a date/time period. After two days of training on relevant concepts and data collection techniques, two teams (representing capture and recapture, respectively) composed of four graduate research assistants of varied nationalities and disciplines, but spanning the same eight languages, set out to comb information sources for cases of trafficking, mostly through Internet searches. When a case was identified, the researcher coded it across 72 variables and recorded the information in a specialized database. After three months of research, the two teams' databases were matched to identify how many cases had been identified by both teams. Like WFF, the data was stratified, but in a less complex manner that focused solely on geography, type of forced labor, and whether data was based on one offense or from an aggregated case source. Finally, statistical modeling was applied to extrapolate from this the total number of forced labor cases, with consideration of stock, the number of victims of forced labor at a specific moment, versus flow, the number of victims moving in and out of situations of forced labor in a broader period of time.

An initial question provoked by the ILO methodology is why the margin of error given (20.9 + 1.4 million) is at the 68 percent level of confidence, as opposed to the more standard 95 percent level, which would require an additional standard deviation from the given estimate. In terms of methodology, ILO was careful to acknowledge the ways in which its approach may have challenged some of the necessary assumptions of capture-recapture sampling. For example, researchers are not working in a closed universe of cases; new reports appear constantly on the Internet, their main source for information. Nor is the likelihood of identifying cases equal across the board. A case reported in the TIP Report by the US Department of State is more likely to be found by researchers than a report from a small, local NGO, particularly if the latter report was not published online. Moreover, the report assumes independence between the two sampling teams, but this is questionable being that they are similarly trained and likely to find the same source material for cases. Furthermore, what one team finds may affect what the other team finds, whether because additional page views and the passage of time affect placement on a search engine results page or because a given NGO has been asked to provide reports which are now handy should the second team contact them. The likelihood of a case being discovered by both teams is higher than the unconditional probability due to a correlation between their samples. Apart from the issues of limiting the samples to only eight languages and emphasizing use of the Internet, thus potentially excluding significant local NGO documentation, there is an additional problem: the numbers derived from single incident reports were likely counted in aggregated reports, leading to double counting (a major challenge in estimating hidden populations generally). The assumptions necessary for a robust prevalence estimate to be derived from capture-recapture methods are simply too stringent. There is no chance that all members of a population of forced laborers have equal probability of being captured. Imagine, for example, a case covered by the *New York Times* as opposed to a case only picked up in a local newspaper, or a highly publicized case with many Google hits compared to a case that appears in a print newsletter report from a small NGO. The report draws attention to these challenges to accurately measuring hidden populations: "It would be unrealistic to expect global estimation of forced labor with a high degree of accuracy."[27] While such self-awareness is commendable, it brings up again an issue that neither global estimate addresses, which is the more fundamental question of why global prevalence measures are necessary in the first place.

It is encouraging, though, that the ILO has an eye on strengthening the robustness of their estimates through its new Data Initiative on Modern Slavery, which was launched last year. In April, a workshop was convened to begin delineating and evaluating existing tools and methodologies applied to surveys on modern slavery used for global estimates. As the initiative develops, its findings will inform a new global estimate of forced labor (expected in 2017, perhaps with regional breakdowns on prevalence) and the implementation by 2016 of a Global Slavery Observatory. This latter initiative aims to be a global database to manage and share qualitative and quantitative information on modern slavery, including tracking anti-trafficking policy changes, through collaboration with other organizations collecting similar data. Initiatives such as this, which identify, accumulate, and share data on a wider and more sustained basis, are necessary and welcomed steps to producing more accurate information on trafficking.

US TIP REPORT

Though not a trafficking prevalence measure, the annual Trafficking in Persons Report produced by the Office to Monitor and Combat Trafficking in Persons at the US Department of State warrants discussion because of its global influence. The TIP Report claims to be the "world's most comprehensive resource of governmental anti-human trafficking efforts."[28] In addition to offering country-by-country narratives, the report ranks each nation on one of three tiers (plus a Tier 2 Watch List), based largely on its government's anti-trafficking policies.

Contents are informed by material coming from US embassies, foreign government officials, local and international NGOs, news articles, academic scholarship, media reports, and information submitted directly to the J/TIP office through an open email system. Tier rankings are largely based on a given government's efforts to comply with the US Trafficking Victims Protection Act's (TVPA) minimum standards for the elimination of human trafficking, rather than evaluating the nature and scope of the issue in the given state. These TVPA standards incorporate numerous provisions, including the passage of relevant laws prohibiting trafficking, minimum punishments for convicted traffickers, the implementation of proactive victim identification mechanisms for frontline law enforcement and service providers, and efforts to provide victims with social and legal services. Therefore, a Tier 1 ranking implies not that human trafficking is not a problem in the place under investigation, but that the government is making efforts to address it in accordance with TVPA, and must continue to do so in order to maintain the ranking. Tier 2 indicates a country that is not fully complying with TVPA's minimum standards, but is making significant efforts to do so. Countries are placed on the Tier 2 Watch List if the number of victims of trafficking is very significant or steadily increasing, if the government cannot provide evidence of increasing efforts from the previous year, or if a government commits to, but has not yet demonstrated, such progress. Tier 3 countries are found noncompliant with TVPA and are not making significant efforts to comply. After two consecutive years on the Tier 2 Watch List, a country that does not improve is automatically downgraded to Tier 3. This policy was introduced in the 2013 TIP Report, though the provision can be waived by the Secretary of State for up to two years if the given government shows strong intentions to comply with TVPA, expressed by implementing a written plan. A waiver, for example, was granted to Thailand in 2012 and 2013 before the state was downgraded to Tier 3 in the 2014 TIP Report (where it remains in 2015).

In addition to avoiding public embarrassment and scorn from the international community, countries are inclined to avoid restrictions on non-humanitarian, non-trade bilateral assistance that can be triggered by a Tier 3 ranking. For example, in the wake of its second consecutive year on Tier 3, Thailand significantly ramped up an anti-trafficking campaign, resulting in a number of arrests, as part of its efforts to be upgraded in 2016.[29] Furthermore, the implicated government would face US opposition to assistance from international financial institutions like the World Bank. However, the president of the United States has the discretion to waive any or all of the sanction provisions to avoid detrimental effects to vulnerable populations or if it is in US national interest to do so.

The TIP Report has drawn widespread critique centered on the inconsistency of data collected and reported, the challenges inherent to such global ranking mechanisms, and the politicization of the issue of human trafficking. Because J/TIP relies highly on self-reported data from governments, NGOs, and other international and local sources, there is little standardization of data, making comparisons and generalizations difficult—an issue that resonates throughout this report. Moreover, because governments have to self-report data, there are incentives to potentially alter the information. Past TIP Reports have put forth global prevalence numbers and/or given estimates as to the number of people trafficked each year, often without concrete citations or explanations of how such numbers were derived, but J/TIP seems to be moving away from this practice. The last reference to prevalence can be found in the 2013 TIP Report: "In contrast, social scientists estimate that as many as 27 million men, women, and children are trafficking victims at any given time."[30]

Like the GSI, the TIP Report is produced with good intentions. Over time, improvements have been made, including broadening the geographical scope. While the report initially evaluated only countries determined to send, receive, or transit "a significant number" of victims of trafficking, it now covers 188 countries and territories, including an introspective look at the United States' own record. Also, the US government has moved beyond the myopic tendency to focus on trafficking of women and girls for the purpose of sexual exploitation—certainly not the only entity guilty of this simplistic narrative—to encompass myriad forms of trafficking, including cases that do not involve physical movement. There seems to be a growing awareness at J/TIP that successful anti-trafficking policies will require more than the development of a legal framework; the implementation of such laws and normative shifts are increasingly highlighted in country narratives.

One of the TIP Report's minimum requirements of foreign governments is that they report information on trafficking investigations, prosecutions, and convictions to the US government; such data is included in the report. Of course, these numbers cannot be used as a proxy for trafficking prevalence as they are reflective of not only the incidence of trafficking, but also government commitment to the issue and state capacity to enforce anti-trafficking laws and judicial processes. Moreover, a change from year to year could reflect either a change in the scale of trafficking or a change in a state's ability to address it.

Besides the obvious challenge of relying on self-reported data to be accurate, this approach has promoted an overemphasis on the criminal justice aspects of trafficking. Its prominence has arguably been detrimental to a more comprehensive structure that ensures survivors receive the resources and services promised by international law, and that governments are working on preventive measures to address vulnerability factors. Still, a fair amount of anecdotal evidence supports the claim that the TIP Report wields considerable influence in shaping the global anti-trafficking agenda, as previously noted. Moreover, NGOs in the field indicated that the report serves as an effective advocacy tool in their work, allowing them to approach the relevant government with specific targets to improve its TIP Report ranking. Not For Sale CEO David Batstone noted in the *Guardian*: "Governments do not want a bad showing in the TIP Report, so targeted strategies looking at how they can work on their anti-trafficking programs using TIP as a framework will often have more of an impact."[31]

Despite healthy criticism, Gallagher asserted in 2011 that the TIP Reports, assuming they are not impeding the development of a potentially superior mechanism, have enriched the conversation: "Without the reports, our collective knowledge of trafficking-related exploitation would likely be less; individual governments would likely have greater control over the flow of information that properly belongs in the public domain; and even the most egregious failure on the part of a state to deal with trafficking-related exploitation would likely come at little reputational or other cost."[32] Of course, improvements can always be made, and just as J/TIP hopes that the naming and shaming element of a poor ranking might positively affect a government's approach, the international community can hope that healthy debate and critique can likewise improve the reporting process.

UNODC GLOBAL REPORT ON TRAFFICKING IN PERSONS

On the tenth anniversary of the adoption of the Protocol to Prevent, Suppress and Punish Trafficking in Persons, Especially Women and Children (Palermo Protocol), member states demonstrated renewed energy on the subject by adopting the United Nations Global Plan of Action to Combat Trafficking in Persons. Among other provisions, this plan, mandated by the United Nations Office on Drugs and Crime (UNODC), was established to collect information and publish a Global Report on Trafficking in Persons every two years. The hope was to enhance the documentation provided by states to the UNODC, as keepers of the Palermo Protocol and the parent Convention on Transnational Organized Crime. It was noted at the time that, "reporting rates are low, and the information received from governments is uneven, shallow, and often ambiguous."[33]

The second iteration of the Global Report on Trafficking in Persons was released in 2014, offering an overview of the state of human trafficking by region based on information gathered from/in 128 countries. It is significant—and deliberate—that the report does not provide country-by-country analyses. Instead, it relies on general discussions of patterns in trafficker and trafficked population demographics, forms of exploitation, flows, typology of the organizational elements of trafficking as a crime, and the response of the international community to this issue.

Based on feedback from a meeting with independent academics and researchers on measuring hidden populations, the UNODC made a very conscious decision *not* to offer a global estimate of trafficking victims. To their minds, the currently available data "do not support the development of a reliable global victim estimate based upon a sound methodology."[34] This conclusion by UNODC supports the above assertion that such global estimates must be treated with considerable caution. Instead, the UNODC plans to focus on a series of limited field-prevalence studies aimed at specific regions and forms of trafficking, and grounded in carefully defined indicators of trafficking relevant to the situation under investigation. Questionnaires and sampling design will be carefully selected for the target context. The expert consultants further encouraged piggybacking on existing data collection vehicles, such as national surveys or other UN-led surveys, where possible.

UNODC research expert Fabrizio Sarrica, a core member of the report team, emphasized this point in a recent interview. "It is clear we are not capturing the dark figure, but we are aware of that limitation," he said. "Our approach is to talk about the things that we know, while being very clear and transparent about the methodology and its limits. There is not an agreed scientific methodology to estimate number of victims of trafficking."[35] Such frankness and modesty in acknowledging the limits of what can and cannot be known with any certainty is a helpful step in identifying suitable methodologies and approaches. Nonetheless, the kind of information provided by UNODC on detected victims is helpful in better understanding profiles, routes, and other elements of trafficking. UNODC plans to expand on this by weaving additional profile pieces into the report, based on qualitative and ethnographic studies.[36]

From an advocacy perspective, the utility of such global reports and, more specifically, prevalence measures is obvious. Each year, the release of these reports generates widespread media coverage and, in turn, public awareness. Yet the question of why we need a global "guesstimate" is rarely asked. Gallagher drew attention to this point in her article "Human Rights and Human Trafficking: A Reflection on the Influence and Evolution of the U.S. Trafficking in Persons Reports," published in 2011. She emphasized that the field could be improved through an acknowledgment of "the well-known problems and pitfalls associated with quantifying the extent of the trafficking problem and the limits of current knowledge." She argued further: "Such an admission could operate as a counterweight to the current unhealthy and unhelpful fixation on numbers and statistics that appears to be an endemic affliction of intergovernmental agencies, NGOs, researchers, and academics working in this area."[37] This perspective alludes to the need for healthy debate as to what global anti-trafficking reports should aim to accomplish and how they may best achieve those goals.

Localized Prevalence Studies: Examples from Southeast Asia

The challenges of global prevalence estimates point to the utility of designing studies with a more narrowed geographical and thematic scope, whether a specific form of trafficking (e.g., child begging, sex trafficking, forced marriage) or a given industry known for high prevalence (e.g., textiles, fishing, electronics). Given that the stated objective of prevalence measures is to assess patterns among trafficked populations and evaluate the impact of policy responses, it only seems logical to focus prevalence measures at a more local level. An effective intervention for curbing sex trafficking in Southern Europe may not apply in West Africa, for example. More focused studies also offer a better understanding of the local context, and allow for more rigorous methodology that is less reliant on extrapolation and assumptions. Moreover, in the process of gathering prevalence data, it is likely that local trafficking patterns will emerge, allowing for better-informed, more targeted interventions. This ethos is beginning to permeate Southeast Asia, where local prevalence studies have been undertaken by multilateral agencies and NGOs. While the scope and robustness of these studies vary, the following examples highlight what is hopefully a growing trend toward replicable, localized prevalence measures.

UN INTER-AGENCY PROJECT ON HUMAN TRAFFICKING—HUMAN TRAFFICKING SENTINEL SURVEILLANCE, POIPET

The United Nations Inter-Agency Project on Human Trafficking (UNIAP, now the United Nations Action for Cooperation Against Trafficking in Persons, or UNACT) issued a series of Sentinel Surveillance reports aimed at assessing local prevalence of trafficking throughout the Greater Mekong Subregion over the course of its mandate. This particular analysis focused on studying the border crossing at Poipet, Cambodia. The objective was to assess the situation of Cambodian deportees returning from Thailand and to estimate numbers and types of cross-border trafficking victims, among other concerns.

Over a period of four months in 2009, researchers carried out site surveys and interviews with a random sample of 400 male and female Cambodian labor migrants deported from Thailand through Poipet.[38] Researchers selected each third person in the reentry processing line for interview, provided that three screening criteria were met—the person provided informed consent, was aged 16 or older, and had just returned from working in Thailand. Poipet was chosen as it receives the "vast majority of all deportees from Thailand." Researchers hypothesized that this population of deportees contained both trafficked and nontrafficked migrants, and comparison would allow them to "pinpoint risk factors and protective factors."[39]

Through interviews, deportees were identified as "clear trafficking cases," "possible trafficking cases," and "not trafficking cases." Criteria for determining trafficking status relied on Thailand's Scope and Elements of Trafficked Persons, which uses definitions in line with the Palermo Protocol. Data analysts compared and contrasted populations deemed to be trafficked and nontrafficked to determine the risk factors that led migrants into harm, and the factors that helped migrants avoid exploitation.[40] Based on their observations of those deportees who had been trafficked among all returning Cambodian migrants crossing the border—23 percent in this case—researchers extrapolated prevalence of trafficking generally, based on official records of deportations.

Obviously this methodology, like any evaluating a hidden population, is imperfect. It is possible that trafficking survivors return to their place of origin in ways other than as official deportees, for example. There may also be significant seasonal variation, especially in regard to labor trafficking, which is not represented in the four-month survey period. Furthermore, conducting interviews at a border crossing likely requires some complicity from the state, which may be difficult to ascertain, and the presence of state officials may intimidate returning trafficked populations. The report recognized some of these limitations, noting that deportees had free choice to opt out of the survey. Some, the report speculates, may have been too traumatized to speak to strangers or afraid to tell the full truth, and others may have exaggerated stories in search of social benefits. "The most significant issue with the methodology is that it only captures deported migrants,"[41] and was not fully representative of the entire Cambodian migrant population. The notoriously porous nature of the Thailand-Cambodia border further complicates this challenge. Therefore, the report recognizes the numerical findings as minimum estimates. Overall, though, this is a move in the right direction as the study sets out clear parameters for the population being studied and relies less heavily on extrapolation compared to global studies. The use of primary data collection, as opposed to newspaper or NGO reports, is further encouraging.

INTERNATIONAL JUSTICE MISSION—CSEC PREVALENCE IN CAMBODIA

With offices in nearly 20 countries worldwide, International Justice Mission (IJM) focuses on rescue (the merits of this element of their anti-trafficking work can be debated, but that is outside the scope of this research), aftercare, and prosecution related to trafficking and sexual exploitation. Earlier this year, IJM released the results of their second study on the prevalence of commercial sexual exploitation of children (CSEC) in Cambodia. They found a significant decrease in the overall percentage of sex workers who are children, which dropped from 8.16 percent in 2012 to 2.2 percent in 2015, according to the study. The findings are based on a variant of time-space sampling conducted through undercover investigation by IJM staff and trained volunteers, most of whom are trained in law enforcement, in the cities of Phnom Penh, Sihanoukville, and Siem Reap.

The findings elicited some controversy from other anti-trafficking organizations, including Agape International Missions, whose executive director questioned the report's accuracy in a *Washington Post* editorial. He indicated that the trade had simply moved further underground, saying that "it's evolved and become more covert."[42] The head of IJM's investigative team in Cambodia, John Roberts, acknowledged this point in a recent interview, but stressed that the government's more stringent approach to CSEC is working to make perpetrators realize it is a riskier business than before.

From a social science perspective, the use of undercover tactics is questionable from both an ethical and methodological standpoint, since researchers' claims cannot be validated and consent cannot be granted from their subjects. That said, IJM offers a thorough and well-articulated description of its research methodology, developed in collaboration with Philippine professor and national statistician

Lisa Grace Bersales. The methodology incorporates consideration of available techniques for measuring hidden populations, careful training for undercover surveyors, and a comprehensive mapping exercise of potential CSEC hubs. (However, it should be considered that as the CSEC industry becomes more hidden, it is less likely that the IJM team will be able to identify all potential places of exploitation.) On a related note, in Cambodia, IJM is prioritizing knowledge sharing by implementing a series of biannual voluntary surveys with civil society and government agencies on how and to what extent they have served victims of sex trafficking. The hope is to equip law enforcement, the judiciary, and social workers with better information so they can address trafficking more proactively and sustainably. With support from the National Committee for Counter Trafficking (NCCT) and the Cambodian National Police, IJM plans to aggregate the survey results to share with relevant government and NGO stakeholders, while maintaining confidentiality.

VERITÉ—FORCED LABOR IN THE PRODUCTION OF ELECTRONIC GOODS IN MALAYSIA

Verité, an international NGO focused on fair labor practices, recently released a two-year study of labor conditions in electronics manufacturing in Malaysia. The report concludes that one in three foreign workers surveyed in the Malaysian electronics industry was in a condition of forced labor. Results are based on interviews with about 500 workers across seven regions of the country covering various products and worker nationalities. In an effort to better understand root causes of this phenomenon, the report highlights key factors that contribute to human rights abuses in this manufacturing sector, including frequent reliance on third-party agents for recruitment, management, and employment of foreign workers; unlawful retention of identification materials; the charging of steep (and often hidden) recruitment fees; and inadequate legal protections.

The study relies on mixed methods, combining both quantitative and qualitative desk research and fieldwork. For the latter portion, Verité combined snowball sampling and quota sampling (also a non-probability technique in which the sample attempts to proportionally recreate the perceived characteristics of the entire population) to intentionally target participants likely or known to have characteristics relevant to situations of forced labor. A team of a dozen researchers representing diverse nationalities and language skills sought out a seed group of recruits. These recruits came from the researchers' existing contacts in the industry, as well as through approaching people at identified gathering places and then asking for referrals to others who might meet inclusion criteria. Once a person was determined to meet given criteria, participants were surveyed to determine if they were in a situation of forced labor. The survey was developed by Verité specifically for this project, and was based on the framework for defining forced labor detailed in the ILO's *Hard to See, Harder to Count* guidelines (see Appendix 2). In addition, the survey was vetted and piloted by the organization's international team.

Verité constructed a thoughtful methodology and offers a detailed explanation of the process in its final report. The research team underwent several weeks of training prior to the fieldwork, including careful review of the research design and methods, with a focus on informed consent and confidentiality, interview skills, data management, and security concerns. In addition, the team was given a clear understanding of the survey instrument and instructions on ensuring consistency in its use, as well as a review of electronics manufacturing processes in general. Unfortunately, based on the non-probability nature of the sampling technique, the results of Verité's study cannot be extrapolated to represent the population of electronics manufacturing laborers at large. Hence, the conclusions reflect characteristics and proportions only of "workers in the study sample."[43] Despite this limitation, the study provides helpful insights into the population of foreign workers in the electronics manufacturing industry in Malaysia that could improve recruitment and employment policies. Moreover, Verité demonstrates an awareness of the biases introduced through survey sampling generally, as well as the statistical limitations of snowball sampling. While acknowledging that the method is imperfect, such studies can still produce valuable data.

CHAB DAI—BUTTERFLY LONGITUDINAL RESEARCH PROJECT

Though not a prevalence measure, Cambodia-based Chab Dai's work on trafficking victim re/integration should be highlighted for its dedication to ethical and rigorous standards. Furthermore, the organization's 10-year Butterfly Longitudinal Research Project is highly unique in the field for its protracted timeframe. Founder and Director Helen Sworn noted that it took significant time to find a donor to fund this research, drawing attention to the underfunding of research on human trafficking generally. (See Appendix 3 for more information on how Chab Dai hopes to incorporate data from this study into a shared, public database.)

The study's mid-point progress report reveals interesting data on survivors' relationships with their families and communities, as well as changes in socioeconomic conditions for themselves and their families.[44] For the first four years of the study, Chab Dai was mostly concerned with collecting quantitative information on survivor demographics, but soon realized that the numbers were not matching up year to year. For example, a survivor's age was not increasing appropriately with the passage of time or information they reported about conditions at the time of trafficking was changing. As a result, the organization decided to shift focus to more qualitative information, thus ensuring accuracy and allowing for more open-ended answers.[45] While researchers had formerly conducted statistical analysis with SPSS software, they now focus on thematic papers based on key commonalities revealed by survivors in interviews. What is most notable about Chab Dai's work is the attention it pays to more stringent methodological and normative standards. For example, Cambodia Country Director Yeng Ros noted that the organization is very careful to build trust with its clients, thus ensuring more accurate reporting. Interviews take place outside of clients' homes to help avoid questions and stigma associated with trafficking, and female interviewers are always assigned to work with female clients. Moreover, staff and consultants are offered intensive training on how to conduct interviews and analyze data, which supplements their academic training in the social sciences.

———————————————————

Though not comprehensive, the above sampling of local prevalence measures undertaken in Southeast Asia provides ideas for potential avenues of exploration as NGOs and governments operating in the region consider undertaking similar studies. While the original intention of this research was to analyze such studies and their resulting prevalence measures, field interviews pointed to the need for more foundational issues to be addressed (with acknowledgment of progress over the past decade) before a methodological critique could really be helpful. Those observations are discussed in the following section.

Toward Robust Data Collection in ASEAN

Equipped with an understanding of currently available research methodologies and how they are employed in the field of human trafficking, the logical next step is to assess the operating environment and potential in ASEAN to implement robust data collection and analysis on prevalence. In 2006, ASEAN and the International Organization for Migration (IOM) partnered on *ASEAN and Trafficking in Persons: Using Data as a Tool to Combat Trafficking in Persons,* a study that then-ASEAN Secretary General Ong Keng Yong hoped would "support the development of appropriate, accurate, and sustainable data collection on such trafficking in ASEAN."[46] Based on research in Cambodia, Indonesia, the Philippines, and Thailand, the report set out to catalog and assess the efforts of ASEAN member states (AMS) to collect trafficking data.

This current research piece initially set out with the same ambition, using the IOM study as a benchmark. However, much as IOM researchers noted in their study a decade ago, the author encountered low to moderate levels of awareness among AMS and NGO practitioners concerning the manner and scope of existing data collected in case studies of Cambodia, Indonesia, and Thailand. Initial discussions in the field pointed toward more basic challenges that must be surmounted before data collection can be standardized and sustained throughout the region. Standardization is, of course, a precondition for accurate and meaningful prevalence studies. Thus, the focus of this report necessarily shifted to delineating where normative, methodological, and technical advancements have been made, and where gaps remain.[47] The following summary observations are based on the experience of NGOs and government agencies in Cambodia, Indonesia, and Thailand. Although believed to be loosely representative of general trends in the region, it should be remembered that each country—and even every locality within a given country— has a unique experience. This awareness supports extending methodologically sound prevalence studies as widely as possible within ASEAN, rather than relying on generalizations from one country to another. Given that trafficking in Southeast Asia is internal, intraregional, and global in scope, the exclusion of some AMS necessarily renders the study incomplete in important ways.

Furthermore, as a reminder that the challenges addressed herein are universal and should not be seen as unfairly targeting practices of governments and NGOs in Southeast Asia, a report issued by the US National Institute of Justice in 2013 draws attention to these very challenges at home. With estimates ranging widely between 14,500 and 50,000 people trafficked annually into the United States, the report concludes that "the data used to estimate the prevalence of human trafficking in the US are lacking in scope and quality at the federal, state, and local levels."[48] These findings are based not only on the hidden nature of the trafficked population, but also on similar challenges of local law enforcement and communities not prioritizing the issue, negative stereotypes about victims, and lack of dedicated resources, according to the study. Again, lack of sufficient and robust data on trafficking is a global, not just regional, challenge.

DEFINITION

Any kind of standardization of data on human trafficking must rely at its most elemental level on a common definition of the problem and its component parts. To put it simply, in the words of one trafficking expert interviewed, "sloppy definitions lead to sloppy research, which in turn leads to sloppy and ineffective policy implementation." This is an area where much progress has been made over the past decade in Southeast Asia, as more countries have ratified the Palermo Protocol and its definition of trafficking has rather widely been adopted as the international standard. Since the 2006 IOM study, which highlighted the challenge of inconsistent definitions, five additional ASEAN nations have ratified or acceded to the Palermo Protocol. By mandating that this trafficking definition be translated into domestic criminal law, the Palermo Protocol helps with the issue of standardization, despite varying degrees of clarity achieved across AMS.[49] Brunei and Singapore remain the only two AMS that have not ratified. This problem could be ameliorated through ratification of the forthcoming ASEAN Convention on Trafficking in Persons (to be discussed in further detail below), which is expected to adopt the Palermo Protocol definition as the regional standard, according to sources close to its development. Several entities interviewed noted the helpfulness of the definition in identifying trafficking cases, particularly by applying the action, means, and purpose elements of the definition (or action and purpose for minors): "We look for the three components—our staff knows this clearly," said the director of a Cambodian NGO working on the issue.

From the Protocol to Prevent, Suppress and Punish Trafficking in Persons, Especially Women and Children, supplementing the United Nations Convention against Transnational Organized Crime

Adopted and opened for signature, ratification, and accession by General Assembly resolution 55/25 of November 15, 2000.

For the purposes of this Protocol:

(a) "Trafficking in persons" shall mean the recruitment, transportation, transfer, harbouring or receipt of persons, by means of the threat or use of force or other forms of coercion, of abduction, of fraud, of deception, of the abuse of power or of a position of vulnerability or of the giving or receiving of payments or benefits to achieve the consent of a person having control over another person, for the purpose of exploitation. Exploitation shall include, at a minimum, the exploitation of the prostitution of others or other forms of sexual exploitation, forced labour or services, slavery or practices similar to slavery, servitude or the removal of organs;

(b) The consent of a victim of trafficking in persons to the intended exploitation set forth in subparagraph (a) of this article shall be irrelevant where any of the means set forth in subparagraph (a) have been used;

(c) The recruitment, transportation, transfer, harbouring or receipt of a child for the purpose of exploitation shall be considered "trafficking in persons" even if this does not involve any of the means set forth in subparagraph (a) of this article;

(d) "Child" shall mean any person under eighteen years of age.

That is not to say that the definition challenge has been solved by the Palermo Protocol. There remains uncertainty about undefined subsidiary concepts, such as "abuse of a position of vulnerability" and associated evidentiary issues, for example. Also, there is an increasing tendency in the anti-trafficking community to conflate terms like modern-day slavery (undefined in international law), slavery, forced labor, and human trafficking, making it difficult for international agreement on a precise definition. Still, there is much value in subscribing to the shared understanding of trafficking in persons offered by the protocol, and perhaps the seeming malleability of the Palermo definition will allow for a broadened definition that better encapsulates larger concepts of exploitation. "There is a need for an increasingly common understanding of human trafficking, and if Palermo is the fixed point we are working toward, then we will have to deal with that," said an international trafficking expert working closely with the Cambodian government. "Going back now will probably result in a more fragmented environment." Fortunately, as more and more countries adopt this definition and begin to adjudicate trafficking cases under that concept, the legislation, government regulations, and jurisprudence will likely expand its definition. As another expert source commented, "how we understood trafficking 10 years ago will be different from our understanding 10 years from now."

Despite this progress, adoption of a common definition in international and domestic law is not a guarantor that anti-trafficking measures will be successfully implemented. The de jure/de facto gap—what is dictated in law versus what happens in reality—is quite evident in Southeast Asia's anti-trafficking sphere, where a deep understanding of the Palermo Protocol's provisions have not yet permeated as widely as one might hope. "They know it, but they don't apply it," was a common sentiment expressed in interviews. "I have spoken to officials in the anti-trafficking division of the Thai police who clearly do not understand the definition," said an international NGO representative. A US government representative noted varying interpretations of what constitutes trafficking across Indonesia, making centralized data collection difficult. (The geography of Indonesia's vast archipelago is a further complicating factor.) In the end, a definition that is commonly adopted, understood, and implemented will be critical to collecting standardized trafficking data on a state, regional, and international basis. Without it, the ability of border officials, police, immigration authorities, and other first responders and service providers to properly identify victims will be hindered. Fortunately, as discussed below, NGOs and governments are making significant public advocacy efforts, as well as offering more targeted law enforcement and justice sector trainings, to ensure this knowledge permeates widely.

A corollary to establishing a common definition of human trafficking is the need for common practices to identify its victims.[50] In addition to adopting (and implementing) a common definition, government coordination is desperately needed to establish a common set of indicators to identify victims of trafficking. Among NGOs interviewed, there seems to be a growing awareness of this need, and several standardized forms for identification have been implemented. Moreover, many of these organizations conduct trainings on victim identification with anti-trafficking police units throughout the region. On the whole, though, these specialized modules have yet to be integrated into standard onboarding of all new officers. Though the IOM and various UN agencies have worked with the government of Indonesia to try to create standardized forms for victim identification, the author was told that such forms are simply created and not put into standard use. In Cambodia, the Ministry of Social Affairs has been developing a national standard for victim identification for the past eight years; the project currently awaits approval from the anti-trafficking task force. Thailand produced a pamphlet in conjunction with the adoption of the national anti-trafficking law of 2008, though its contents appear rather nebulous and difficult to translate into day-to-day operations.[51]

POLITICAL WILL

To achieve lasting progress in combating human trafficking—a process requiring massive national and regional collaboration, as well as dedicated resources for standardized data collection—ASEAN governments will have to exercise tremendous political will and leadership. Appropriate budgets need to be allocated, civil servants need to be appropriately trained, and advocacy campaigns need to be undertaken to ensure the public is engaged on this issue. All of these elements require strong governance. As the issue of human trafficking gains ever-growing international attention, outward demonstrations expressing commitment to the problem are often made. Though this concern about human trafficking seems to be legitimate—perhaps triggered by both a realization of the domestic challenges the problem poses, as well as a desire to avoid international censure—nearly every source interviewed, both in and outside government, questioned the depth of political will required to facilitate the collaboration and dedicate the resources necessary to truly combat trafficking in persons.

Many regional practitioners and experts pointed, once again, to the chasm between what is promised and what is implemented. In some cases, the gap translates into robust laws and policies on the issue of trafficking—for example, Indonesia's National Law 21/2007 is highly regarded for its definition of exploitation that goes beyond the Palermo Protocol—but, "there is a real problem with implementation," noted one source, a sentiment shared by many. Another NGO representative opined that the government "is happy to turn a blind eye to trafficking if it means you can reduce unemployment and social problems at home." On the other hand, partly in response to public pressure, the Indonesian government has developed significant initiatives to attempt to deal with the plight of Indonesians working abroad in countries such as Saudi Arabia and Malaysia. Several other interviewees noted deep dissatisfaction with the Thai government's response to the issue, despite very strong public speeches from the prime minister, who recently urged that "all state agencies must be serious about implementing the existing laws....All elements supporting human trafficking must be eliminated."[52]

If budget allocations are one reflection of government priorities, then commitment appears rather limited. Though hard numbers are difficult to come by in the field, both governmental and nongovernmental sources noted that the paucity of available funds for their work and lack of coordination often lead to inefficiencies. As an example, in Cambodia, a source working with the NCCT indicated that a request had recently been made for additional funds, beyond the $100,000 per annum that typically pays for staff, rent, and little else. They are still awaiting budget approval. In another example, when an anti-trafficking police force was established there in 2002, it received no additional resources or training beyond the standard police budget, said one source. A locally operated NGO with significant experience working with local police noted how little funding it would take to help these units operate more effectively, estimating the cost in the tens of thousands of dollars, yet they are simply not allocated additional funds. In fact, he reported that the average anti-trafficking unit gets $25 per month to conduct operations. Given these meager sums, NGOs are often relied on to supply basic operating expenses for these units, such as office supplies or travel costs to conduct investigations. This process creates a perverse incentive for governments to neglect their anti-trafficking forces: "As long as NGOs like us keep paying, they don't have to make the investment," the source noted. The NGOs, on the other hand, cannot simply cut off funding for fear the work may stop altogether.

On the issue of data collection, this apparent lack of commitment is reflected in the minimal amount of trafficking information available at the central government level. "Generally, data is terrible," quipped the director of a multilateral agency working in the region. Field contacts mentioned the existence of seemingly random sources of incomplete data, with little effort made to ensure comparability. "Different ministries all have different sources of information so they report different numbers," a government source in Indonesia noted. A further challenge is lack of coordination on cases, which means that double counting of cases reported by various ministries is a common issue in all three countries. For example, the police may have data on trafficking investigations, but there is often little coordination with the attorney general or justice ministries to track the progress of those investigations, and whether suspected traffickers are eventually prosecuted.

If any information is available, it is typically related to the raw number of traffickers arrested, prosecuted, and convicted (the US TIP Report helped to cement this requirement, for better or worse). Moreover, information is highly fragmented, with each ministry implementing its own methods for collecting and keeping records. In Indonesia, the Ministry of Women's Empowerment and Child Protection (KPPPA) gathers data from various ministries and other institutions into an annual report, but a source there indicated that the data is difficult to compare and analyze owing to the nonsystematic collection and reporting process. The ministry also publishes data from anti-trafficking NGOs on victims served, but because reporting is a voluntary process, data is often sparse and incompatible. In addition, information can be difficult or impossible for the public to access, in part because of a lack of emphasis on government transparency. Another multilateral representative with close connections to ASEAN observed: "Data collection in this region is still so limited. There is a long way to go, but it's quite difficult to convince our local partners to do research on this because it's such a sensitive issue."

Another marker of political will is the level of coordination across ministries, assuming that strong commitment from the top would permeate through the bureaucracy. Again, there is a notable gap between the existence of mechanisms to combat trafficking and their ability to function effectively. Despite the presence of coordinating bodies in AMS, nearly every interview noted the lack of coordination across the central government as a major barrier to effective anti-trafficking policies.

In Thailand, two interagency bodies coordinate the work of various ministries on trafficking—the Anti-Trafficking in Persons Committee, which is chaired by the prime minister, and the Coordinating and Monitoring of Anti-Trafficking in Persons Performance Committee, chaired by the deputy prime minster. The former prepares prevention policies, while the latter monitors implementation. Both operate with participation from a wide range of ministerial offices: foreign affairs, social development and human security, the interior, justice, labor, and tourism and sports, for example, as well as outside experts. According to Thailand's 2014 progress report for the J/TIP office, these two bodies met nine times in 2013, yet many still question the efficacy of Thailand's anti-trafficking efforts. In July 2015, the government announced that it will soon establish a new anti-trafficking interagency task force that will include the Royal Thai Police, the Department of Special Investigation, and the Social Development and Human Security Ministry, with support from national anti-corruption entities—a potential indicator of a more robust approach.[53]

Many NGOs in Cambodia expressed much hope for the NCCT, under the deputy chairmanship of Chou Bun Eng. Following a two-year evaluation of its initial National Plan of Action (2011–2013), the six-year-old committee expanded its staff from six to 50 people, who are spread across multiple ministries—interior, justice, labor, social affairs, women's affairs, and education. Though enhanced cooperation is desperately needed between these ministries, a source close to the committee indicated that improvements were expected. A recent decision to require each minister to report directly to the committee would enhance the sense of ownership and responsibility. In the past, this reporting function was often delegated to lower-level civil servants.

In Indonesia, the anti-trafficking task force has existed for more than a decade. However, due largely to a lack of cooperation among its numerous member entities, little seems to come out of it beyond an annual meeting, where representatives report on their respective ministry's anti-trafficking activities from the past year. Multiple sources in Indonesia pointed to the challenge of having the KPPPA serve as secretariat of the anti-trafficking task force. Because of the KPPPA's mandate, it is "not taken seriously" by others in government, though overcoming these arguably chauvinistic attitudes is more a normative challenge than a technical one.

In the long run, the existence of these bodies can be helpful in coordinating anti-trafficking policy and eventually improving data collection. But simply convening a group of people does not automatically lead to measurable outcomes. Notorious rivalries and lack of cooperation between key institutions only exacerbate the problem. While there are obvious challenges to gathering so many entities with competing priorities at the table, the complexity of the issue deserves this kind of multifaceted approach. Successfully implementing anti-trafficking policies is achievable, but it will require clearer mandates for each agency; high-level, centralized direction; and mutual respect for the work that each organization does.

On a related note, an encouraging sign of progress among AMS toward better collaboration is in the development of national action plans. A national action plan is a useful framework to implement a comprehensive and wide-reaching anti-trafficking policy—and its very existence demonstrates some level of commitment to the issue. However, to be truly effective, such a plan must assign relevant tasks to specific government entities with predetermined time lines for implementation and very clear indicators to measure progress. Without this, it is likely that little will be accomplished.

Cambodia shows particular promise in this arena. The NCCT recently released its 2014–2018 National Action Plan, following an in-depth evaluation of the previous plan and heavy consultation with ministries, NGO partners, and experts. The review highlighted achievements in coordinating the work of various ministries and improving public awareness of trafficking, particularly among law enforcement. At the same time, the plan also noted the challenges of implementation, such as a truncated time line (the 2011–2013 plan was not endorsed until February 2012) and lack of budgetary support. Though it is difficult to know if these issues can be effectively addressed with the latest plan, the inclusion of a logic model outlining specific activities linked to desired outcomes and the assignment of lead agencies and timeframes are promising developments. These concrete details should allow for effective monitoring and evaluation to ensure that future plans build on successes and address ongoing challenges. With regard to data collection, the new action plan spells out goals of establishing an information and complaints database concerning labor migration, expanding the trafficking prosecutions database, and creating a national database for trafficking cases.

Indonesia has promised a new action plan since the previous one expired in 2014, and it is said to be in progress. In Thailand, no current national action plan was mentioned in field interviews. However, review of a previous plan compiled for J/TIP revealed little more than a list of aspirational goals, with no clear markers of progress or assignment of specific tasks to relevant ministries.[54] For countries that have not yet developed a national action plan or are looking to strengthen an existing plan, a useful guide could be the 2008 report published by the Organization for Security and Co-operation in Europe, which documents efforts to enhance coordination and reporting mechanisms. The report was prepared by the Office of the Special Representative and Coordinator for Combating Trafficking in Human Beings and is available online.[55]

OVERRELIANCE ON NGO SUPPORT

Despite some signs of mistrust between civil society and governments, interviews also revealed encouraging signs of NGOs and governments working together on the issue of human trafficking, as they have been for some time in certain ASEAN contexts. From resettling trafficking victims to training police officers and prosecutors on the issue, several positive examples of collaboration stood out. However, anecdotes also circulated about NGOs stepping in to essentially fill the role of governments, from providing lawyers for the prosecution of traffickers to being the exclusive source of mental and physical health care and shelter for victims. For example, an Indonesian NGO dedicated to serving irregular migrants cited a case in which a woman migrated internationally under the false pretense that she would be working in a beauty salon, only to find she had been trafficked into sex work. The young woman's mother, upon reporting to the police that she had not heard from her daughter, received no response. She eventually contacted the NGO, which was able to coordinate with the relevant ministries and the foreign embassy to open an investigation. A Cambodian NGO leader lamented the level of resource support his organization is asked to offer the nation's anti-trafficking police force, including gas money or per diems to carry out investigations, computer equipment, or even basic office supplies. "If we don't support them, they cannot do their job." This was a common complaint, particularly in Cambodia. Furthermore, the time and financial resources dedicated to supporting the police take away from the NGOs' own missions and programming. In the end, though, as summarized by a trafficking expert, "it is not the NGOs who are going to enforce law and order." With an issue as complex as standardizing data collection across a state, much less regionally, government commitment and leadership will be required.

One major area where many NGOs have stepped in to assist the government is training anti-trafficking police and prosecutors. Though training in victim identification and best practices for investigating and trying trafficking cases is highly valuable—"we have seen these offices grow substantially in capacity and ability," gushed one NGO—very little work has been done to assess their effectiveness. NGOs and multilateral agencies reported several cases of officers who had been trained multiple times, up to a dozen times, yet police still struggle to process trafficking cases in many contexts. Sources in all three case study countries cited frequent staff turnover as the major challenge to the institutionalization of these trainings, despite undertaking trainings of trainers. "You train them today, and tomorrow they change," said an Indonesian NGO representative. "We are always starting from zero." This challenge of frequent rotation permeates the civil service structure generally. Without sustained commitment to the issue of trafficking, turnover will limit not just the effectiveness of NGO-led trainings, but also the resources allocated to anti-trafficking efforts as officers come and go.

Related to the issue of overreliance on NGO funding, and coupled with inadequate training to support robust research methodology, several contacts noted that past efforts to create national anti-trafficking databases had waned. This problem arises from several sources, but a key issue is that these projects are often donor-driven, and when the program ends and external resources run out, the state cannot or will not take up the workload. This reluctance may stem from capacity issues or limited training, as discussed herein. Another major challenge is that databases are viewed as quick-fix solutions. Little thought is given to design—what data should be collected and why? The same is true for sustainability—who will enter and analyze the data, and how will they be paid long-term? Obviously, without agreement on standard data points, collection practices, and reporting mechanisms, a trafficking database will simply not function. (See Appendix 3 for an outline of existing human trafficking databases.)

For example, in Cambodia, USAID supported the creation of a database for provincial courts to report trafficking case information to the central level. When the project period was over, local courts stopped providing data, according to a multilateral agency working there. The 2006 IOM report also alluded to the creation of a meta-database, Child-Protection.info, to address some of the challenges of establishing common definitions and standardizing data from multiple agencies. However, almost a decade later, there is no indication that such a mechanism has been created and no interviewees had information to offer when questioned.

Similarly, Thailand planned to implement an integrated electronic database, BACKBONE, to consolidate data from and enhance communication between various government agencies. A source familiar with the project indicated that, although the government claims to have developed it, there is no evidence of its existence. This claim could not be verified with the Thai government.

In Indonesia, primary data does not seem to be collected at the central government level, except by the Indonesian National Police, which collects data from various provinces on trafficking cases. Both the Coordinating Ministry of People's Welfare and the KPPPA collate secondary data from various sources, such as other ministries, NGOs, and the media, but that data is not easily comparable because of the non-standardized way in which it is collected. Much like the Cambodian case above, a local NGO described its heavy involvement in a project to enhance the KPPPA's system, yet the project never took off. "There have been a lot of false starts," the director said. A larger international NGO mentioned a similar initiative with KPPPA, but said reports produced from the collated information were difficult to interpret, given the different methodologies used to collect the data.

CORRUPTION

Corruption, the abuse of public power for private gain, plagues every nation across the globe, posing economic, political, and social challenges. With the advent of the ASEAN Economic Community at the end of this year, reigning in such abuse in the region is more critical than ever. Quite simply, human trafficking cannot exist to the degree that it does without corruption, and combatting it is futile if corruption is not also addressed in the relevant institutional contexts. Earlier this year, Transparency International published a report that emphasizes this point, calling for the creation of a regional body aimed at tackling corruption on the eve of ASEAN's economic integration.[56] The organization highlighted a lack of transparency and accountability among public institutions, the absence of key anti-corruption laws, and a tightening civil society space. Only Malaysia and Singapore rank above 50 (on a 0–100 scale) in Transparency International's 2014 Corruption Perceptions Index,[57] and the organization's surveys reveal that half the population of ASEAN believes corruption has increased.[58] The difficulty of capturing trafficking-related corruption in quantitative studies has led organizations like the United Nations to incorporate more qualitative components to their global trafficking reports, according to Fabrizio Sarrica of the UNODC. "Trafficking and corruption are both very difficult to detect—we all know it's happening, but it's not coming up,"[59] he said, noting this has motivated the agency to include specific questions on corruption in their surveys.

Though not all trafficking in Southeast Asia relies on extensive, organized, and illicit networks, widespread corruption exists, from low-level customs officials taking bribes to police officers who accept payoffs in exchange for turning a blind eye to high-level government officials protecting—or, worse, participating in—these networks. Sizeable profits perpetuate their very existence and the past year has seen several reports of corruption related to human trafficking in the region. Fortunately, there is also a growing awareness that the culture of impunity that has long protected such bad actors is untenable.

Thailand's indictment in July 2015 of 72 human trafficking suspects, including one military official, four police officers, and ten other Thai officials, is encouraging. Still, it is somewhat difficult to get past the notion that this is a political move happening just days before the US TIP Report was due to come out. (Thailand has been very vocal about its disappointment at being placed on Tier 3.)[60] The move is the first wave following a widespread investigation that began in May into the "biggest human trafficking" operation in Thailand's history, according to Deputy National Police Chief Aek Angsananont. Additional arrest warrants are outstanding.

These individuals have been charged with crimes ranging from human trafficking and transnational criminal activity to bringing foreign workers into Thailand illegally and violation of official duty. The courts must now decide whether to take up the cases. Despite the arrests, questions have been raised about the long-term effectiveness of Thailand's crackdown on the lucrative trafficking syndicates. A July 2015 *Reuters* investigation showed how the crackdown ran into daunting obstacles, including witness intimidation. Human Rights Watch Deputy Asia Director Phil Robertson acknowledged the increased arrests, but raised concern that high-level officials would remain immune to punishment: "They're not getting to the real masterminds, the sort of senior patrons behind these movements."[61] He expected to see the same pattern of arresting lower-level suspects in Malaysia in the wake of the discovery of trafficking camps on the country's northern border, noting that it would be difficult for such enclaves to exist without official complicity. The Malaysian chief of police, however, has vowed that no one was immune to investigation.[62]

This issue recently came to the fore in Cambodia when it was revealed that the former chief of the Phnom Penh Municipal Anti-Human Trafficking and Juvenile Protection Police, who had been found guilty of trafficking crimes—he was charged as an accomplice to aggravated procurement of prostitution and sentenced to seven years imprisonment—is currently serving as a high-ranking official in the Phnom Penh Municipal Police.[63] The vast reach of the trafficking ring this official was alleged to be involved with was recently revealed by a US State Department cable obtained by the *Phnom Penh Post* through a Freedom of Information Act request. The cable indicated that a sex-trafficking network, which provided cover for Vietnamese sex rings and collected payoffs from illegal prostitution establishments in Cambodia, had enlisted the help of both law enforcement and NGO individuals, who were paid $200–$300 to provide information on upcoming raids.

VICTIMS TREATED AS CRIMINALS

The wrongful conflation of victims with criminals has been an ongoing challenge in the field of human trafficking, and until it is addressed, "counting" victims will remain difficult. Field interviews indicated that this practice is declining, both from a normative and practical sense. However, this is a shift that still requires some attention.

A report from June 2015 about the mass exodus of people from Myanmar and Bangladesh (many of whom had been smuggled as opposed to trafficked) illustrates how the victim/criminal designation can be confused. In this case, Thai authorities jailed a Rohingya woman who had been trafficked, lured into believing she was taking a job in a new city, but was instead sold and placed on a cargo ship headed for the Bay of Bengal. When she arrived in Thailand, she was accused of illegal entry and incarcerated for three months.[64] The ongoing case of Mary Jane Veloso has also drawn attention to this issue. Veloso, a Filipina, faces death row in Indonesia after being convicted, many believe wrongfully, of drug trafficking. Indonesia President Joko Widodo has granted her temporary reprieve so that she can give testimony in a Philippine investigation into the trafficking operation, which Veloso claims victimized her.

Various field interviews called attention to this issue. A common observation critiqued "a mentality of, 'if you are an illegal migrant, you are not a victim.'" Others expressed concern that police interviews are more like interrogations—"they treat victims like perpetrators." Often, survivors are forced to remain in the destination or transit place where they are initially identified, awaiting the initiation of prosecutions before they can return home. During this time, they may be held in prison-like conditions. "I don't see why you can't let them go home and videoconference in from the relevant embassy during the court proceedings," suggested one international NGO employee working in Indonesia.

On a positive note, the notion that human trafficking is linked only to sexual exploitation, and therefore disproportionately affects women and children, seems to be waning in the region. The shift is due, in part, to recent attention around the Benjina scandal, involving hundreds of men enslaved in the fish trade, and other highly publicized instances of labor trafficking and abuse involving men. It is encouraging that the various government task forces previously discussed include diverse ministries, as opposed to relegating the issue only to women's ministries, as was sometimes done in the past. However, challenges still remain. "Throughout the region, there is still a preoccupation with sex trafficking, even though we know labor trafficking is more significant," said a regional expert working in Bangkok. In Indonesia, there is an awareness of the growing number of male victims, but related services are still predominately targeted to women—for example, there are no dedicated shelters for male victims.

LACK OF SKILLS TRAINING

What will arguably remain the largest barrier to effective data collection and analysis on trafficking prevalence in Southeast Asia is the lack of locally available training in social work, research methodologies, and statistics. As a representative of a multilateral agency with familiarity in several Southeast Asian countries indicated: "You're facing very significant capacity restraints here. It is obviously a function of the system in which they operate."

A representative of an anti-trafficking Cambodian NGO, who regularly interviews survivors, noted that her college training in sociology was helpful in the job, but that much of the training has to come directly from the NGO. Degrees in social work are hard to come by, she noted, citing the Royal University as the only Cambodian institution offering graduate-level work in this field. A government representative in Indonesia highlighted the challenge of not having a national certification process for social workers. Only two NGOs consulted mentioned using statistical analytics software like SPSS or STATA to carry out analysis of their data. And one was a large, international entity operating throughout the region, meaning the more in-depth analysis was done at the central level, leaving little opportunity for local capacity building. In this instance, with national consultants carrying out the initial analysis sent up the chain to the home office for a regional report, a head researcher noted that, in hindsight, more training would have been helpful to ensure standardization protocols. Though they were encouraged to carry out analysis beyond what was required, the local researchers "did not have the capacity, neither technical nor in terms of time, to do that."

Several interviewees noted that a mass of data collected was not being used or analyzed in any meaningful way, either because of a shortage of time and staff to devote to such projects or a lack of training to think through proper study methodologies and ensure that the data is high-quality. Several sources lamented "a lot of lost learning opportunities." Other comments reflected similar sentiments: "We need a more systematic and strategic approach toward research projects that allows for local learning." "We need to be collecting better evidence about what does and doesn't work so we can do better programming," commented a government representative.

An exacerbating challenge is simply limited mandates. A US government representative in Jakarta highlighted "pretty good" statistics and political science training among the population, but noted that these skills are rarely put to use on the job. Hence, it seems reasonable that as government agencies and NGOs begin providing more robust training, and academia takes on a larger role, employees will be able to apply such skills to human trafficking research.

TECHNICAL AND NORMATIVE LIMITATIONS TO DATA PROTECTION

Any kind of information collected on human trafficking almost certainly includes very personal details, from names and locations of family members to socioeconomic variables to medical history. As such, it is critical to keep such data protected, particularly considering that many trafficking survivors face intimidation from their former traffickers or stigma in their home communities. (See Appendix 1 for information on ethical and legal considerations of trafficking data, and resources for digital data protection.) On the positive side, some anti-trafficking NGOs consulted for this research noted that there is institutional dedication to keeping data secure. Some put it into practice by password protecting computers on which digital information is stored or allowing only high-level staff to access certain computer files. Those storing hard-copy forms likewise mentioned locked storage cabinets. Several others noted the importance of anonymization when amassing large amounts of data. At least one NGO employed Martus, a secure, open-source data collection and information management tool for human rights practitioners, developed by Silicon Valley–based technology firm Benetech. Overall, though, there seems to be little capacity for data encryption or employment of more secure collection tools. Moreover, much of the information collected is analog—that is, forms are filled out and kept in binders or cabinets, often accessible to anyone in the office. In one government ministry, for example, a binder that documented trafficking survivors—reported by foreign embassies with identifying information, including photographs—was left open on a central table. Generally, addressing this issue requires both a heightened awareness of the potential damage caused by insecure data, as well as improved technical tools for keeping data secure.

In discussing the manner of data collection with government and NGO representatives, it quickly became clear that the technological environment they are operating in is more limited than what might be available elsewhere.[65] That said, the Cambodian National Police have expressed a desire to simplify data transfer from provincial to central levels through the use of mobile applications on smartphones (generally, these transfers happen by fax, phone, or not at all). However, concerns about implementation are being raised, both in terms of data protection and technical capability. For the great majority of entities consulted, trafficking data is collected with pen and paper, perhaps on forms, perhaps just in a notebook, where it might later be transferred to a form and/or an electronic database. If the latter, this is typically a rudimentary electronic spreadsheet or word-processing document. Very few mentioned cloud-based or network storage that allowed multiple users to work within the same set of documents. Instead, the interviewees indicated that files are filled in individually and sent up the organizational chain for further review.

Despite these challenges, a common theme to nearly all queries on human trafficking data collection and analysis was a keen awareness of the potential utility of data—and a desire to improve current practices. If actors across government and civil society could share information and regard each other as partners combatting a common problem, they would better serve the national interest. By coordinating the use of similar metrics and methods, and being willing to share data and resources, the scale and scope of the problem can begin to be grasped. Such national coordination is just the first step. As has already been established, human trafficking continues to pose an economic, political, and social threat to the entire region, and thus an effort toward regional coordination and standardization will be needed to ensure an effective and sustainable response.

A Role for ASEAN

The only way Southeast Asia can have a coordinated regional approach to battling human trafficking is through harmonization of laws, policies, methods, and information exchange. The process of building robust, regional datasets on human trafficking will necessitate an umbrella body working to minimize the substantial differences in national legislative frameworks, identification methods, and collection tools and strategies.

The normative and technical barriers outlined in the previous section draw attention to the need for renewed commitment to anti-trafficking efforts throughout the region. The fact that organizations across sectors and countries pointed to similar fundamental challenges suggests the need for a coordinated response across the region. Several sources agreed that "ASEAN has the most potential to harmonize regional counter-trafficking strategies." Moreover, it is in ASEAN's interest to do so. Without proper preventive strategies, the cementing of the ASEAN Economic Community in 2015—though positive for the region's development—runs the risk of bringing more pernicious consequences for already vulnerable populations.

Fortunately, ASEAN member states have shown willingness, albeit to varying degrees, to participate in multilateral anti-trafficking processes, such as the Coordinated Mekong Ministerial Initiative against Trafficking (COMMIT) and ASEAN-U.S. PROGRESS. Furthermore, ASEAN as a body demonstrated its commitment to the issue of human trafficking over 10 years ago with the Declaration Against Trafficking in Persons Particularly Women and Children. Though nonbinding, signatories pledged to exchange information on trafficking trends, intensify cooperation among relevant agencies, prioritize victim care, and, more generally, "to take measures to strengthen regional and international cooperation to prevent and combat trafficking in persons."[66] To varying degrees, member states have made progress in fulfilling these commitments, as outlined above. In addition, ASEAN as a body has moved toward improved coordination, including by implementing several regional training programs on how to proactively identify victims in at least nine of the 10 AMS.[67] Further examples of these efforts include a regional system established in 2004 to exchange intelligence and best practices among specialist trafficking units in Southeast Asia, implementation of a trafficking case analysis system, and the development of ASEAN Practitioner Guidelines[68] by the Ad-Hoc Working Group on Trafficking in Persons in 2007 to assist the criminal justice agencies of member states.[69]

The regional implications of recent trafficking scandals, such as the discovery of mass graves in Thailand and Malaysia and enslaved fishermen in Indonesia, urgently point to the need for more leadership on the issue, including through collaboration with regional NGOs. Responding to the graves found in trafficking camps, ASEAN Parliamentarians for Human Rights indicated that this is "yet another disturbing outcome of a collective lack of leadership on the part of regional governments to address the pervasive problem of human trafficking."[70] In response to the ongoing crisis of smuggled boat people from Bangladesh and Myanmar, a local United Nations High Commissioner for Refugees spokesperson lamented, "At this point, I'm not sure what the concrete next steps are or should be....But there doesn't seem to be a clear mechanism in this region for responding to something like this."[71]

In terms of data collection specifically, though every country faces unique challenges, the commonalities point to ASEAN's increasingly important role as a regional force in coordinating standardized, robust data collection—and ASEAN has demonstrated an awareness of this fact. In conjunction with the 2006 IOM study on trafficking data in ASEAN, a workshop was convened to discuss the research findings and recommendations for improving the process. Several recommendations were reviewed and adopted by the Senior Officials Meeting on Transnational Crime (SOMTC) Working Group on Trafficking, including the use of a common definition of trafficking; the establishment of focal points on trafficking data reported to SOMTC, including data relevant to prevention, prosecution, and protection, as well as a related template for reporting; an emphasis on the need for training and capacity building; and the creation of a mechanism "for the collection of qualitative and quantitative data to prevent the trafficking in persons."[72] Considering the rather broad and nebulous nature of these recommendations, it is not surprising that little progress has been made in their implementation.

In 2007, the SOMTC was tasked with looking into the development of an ASEAN convention to address trafficking in persons. It then convened an expert working group to draft such a treaty and a corresponding regional plan of action for the convention's operationalization. According to SOMTC participant Felizardo Serapio, head of the Philippines Secretariat and executive director of the Philippine Center for Transnational Crime, after nine meetings and rigorous deliberations over a span of eight years, the expert working group—composed of experts in the field of law enforcement, prosecution, social welfare, international law, and human rights protection from each of the 10 AMS—adopted all the provisions of the working draft. The document purports to provide a regionally agreeable framework for AMS collaboration on criminal justice and victim service provisions, including safe return, rehabilitation, and reintegration of trafficked people into their respective societies.[73]

The forthcoming ASEAN Convention on Trafficking in Persons (ACTIP) will likely cement the Palermo Protocol definition as the accepted definition of trafficking for the region, and focal points have been established. A reliable source indicated that the associated regional plan of action has two major points that address trafficking data collection. One is a provision that each member state should establish a national data collection system that includes a method for sharing data among states, with the ultimate goal of creating a regional database. Second, the plan looks at implementing or supporting research on combatting trafficking generally, with a specific focus on how to better collect appropriate data and encourage more effective analysis. The goal is to improve understanding of the scale and scope of the problem at both a national and regional level.

Though most ASEAN member states have already made similar commitments through ratification of the Palermo Protocol, the ACTIP ensures both a sense of ownership and an awareness of the unique geographical and cultural context in which these countries operate. The forthcoming convention demonstrates serious dedication to this issue as the fourth convention adopted by ASEAN since its founding in 1967 (the others center on amity and cooperation, disaster management, and counterterrorism). But as indicated above, successful implementation will require political will and sustained commitment. The leadership provided by the SOMTC in pushing this convention forward, particularly with minimal international intervention, should be heralded. As has been emphasized throughout this report, though, the complexity of the issue of trafficking requires an ethos of collaboration across fields of expertise. SOMTC members disproportionately represent specific ministry types, such as justice or foreign affairs, making it probable that other points of view, particularly those of more socially oriented institutions, are not being represented. As such, it is unfortunate that other relevant ASEAN bodies—such as the ASEAN Intergovernmental Commission on Human Rights (AICHR), the ASEAN Commission on the Promotion and Protection of the Rights of Women and Children (ACWC), and the ASEAN Committee on the Implementation of the ASEAN Declaration on the Protection and Promotion of the Rights of Migrant Workers (ACMW)—have been sidelined in the drafting process.

As ASEAN implements the trafficking convention and coordinating regional action plan, there are existing instruments the body could look to for potential guidance and lessons learned (see Appendix 2). Furthermore, if implemented, the policy recommendations outlined in the following section will help ensure a robust, coordinated response that will not only allow for improved regional prevalence measures, but also progress toward effectively combatting the pernicious problem of human trafficking.

Policy Recommendations

As established in this report, human trafficking is a complex issue that requires equally multifaceted and well-coordinated solutions. The following policy recommendations are offered to ASEAN, the governments of ASEAN member states, and the international anti-trafficking community with the awareness that a transnational crime like human trafficking requires a robust, regional response, and that progress toward improved prevalence measures will require collaboration across all these entities. ASEAN has long demonstrated its commitment to this issue, and as a respected institution, both in and outside the region, it is uniquely situated to galvanize cooperation and collaboration across member states. Tackling the issue of trafficking provides a unique opportunity for ASEAN to demonstrate its leadership and relevance in the region and across the globe. Thus, the recommendations are focused not only on better prevalence measures, but also on general ways actors across the region can work together on this critical issue.

RECOMMENDATIONS FOR ASEAN

- Because of the frequently international character of human trafficking, the creation of a regional database on trafficking is a logical step toward enhancing the capacity for effective ASEAN initiatives. Rather than relying on international organizations and NGOs, ASEAN "ownership" of the database is likely the only way to secure the AMS cooperation necessary for improving access to quality data. However, careful consideration of what types of data are needed to better measure the scale and scope of the problem, along with coordination on victim identification and data collection standards, will be critical first steps. Data has the potential to be a powerful and illuminating tool, but bad data poorly collected and analyzed can be worse than no data. Creation of an ASEAN working group of experts would be an important starting place to ensure that data collection and analysis are properly designed and implemented.

- Robust and sustainable research and analysis on trafficking prevalence will require heightened awareness of proper methodologies and training in social science research. To ensure long-term sustainability and enhancement of regional capacity, ASEAN should encourage the development of relevant expertise through academic exchange programs and funding to support advanced education. In the meantime, those working with trafficking data must be trained on proper collection techniques, including an awareness of security considerations and privacy laws, as well as given statistical training to better understand what the data can reveal and how to conduct proper analyses. Public-private partnerships, university-based research cooperation, and international and regional collaborations could facilitate the two-way knowledge exchange required for designing robust, culturally relevant research methodologies for future prevalence studies, while guaranteeing more sustainable resource allocation.

- Through collaborative processes such as COMMIT and the Bali Process, ASEAN member states have already demonstrated a willingness to work together on the issue of human trafficking, albeit to varying degrees. ASEAN should gather the points of contacts for these various partnerships for "lessons learned" exchanges that can lead to improved collaboration, effectiveness, and policy formulation in anti-trafficking efforts. Efforts should be directed to developing information-sharing techniques for data on suspects, convicted traffickers, and victims among service providers, law enforcement, judiciaries, relevant ministries, and border control agencies.

- Government complicity in trafficking at any level is guaranteed to impede the collection of reliable trafficking data. As such, an effective approach to combat trafficking in the region must include an anti-corruption component. Despite the obvious political sensitivities in this area, research is required to develop a better understanding of the scope and manner in which corruption facilitates trafficking and impedes anti-trafficking efforts. Especially with the advent of the AEC and ACTIP, the adoption of an ASEAN strategy for dealing with this issue should be a priority.

- In order to ensure the effectiveness of the forthcoming ASEAN Convention on Trafficking in Persons, ASEAN should consider creating a reporting mechanism. One model would be a regional body of experts, perhaps similar to the Council of Europe's Group of Experts on Action against Trafficking in Human Beings, to collect and disseminate information on measures taken by ASEAN member states to implement the ACTIP. The development of such a regional resource would promote ASEAN-based information on compliance and implementation measures, rather than the current reliance on international reports such as the US TIP Report. It would also demonstrate ASEAN's commitment to following up the ACTIP with a regional approach to implementation.

RECOMMENDATIONS FOR THE GOVERNMENTS OF ASEAN MEMBER STATES

- Solving any challenge requires a common understanding of the problem itself. Though most AMS governments are now party to the Palermo Protocol and have come to adopt its definition of human trafficking as their own, more work is needed to ensure this understanding pervades throughout the various central government institutions engaged in anti-trafficking measures, and that it permeates down to activities at the local level. To help promote coordinated responses to trafficking throughout ASEAN, a common set of training and explanatory materials should be adopted, with consideration to unique local circumstances, based on the ACTIP. These materials can then be implemented among social service providers, law enforcement, immigration, the justice sector, and other relevant institutions at the national, regional, and local levels.

- Effective anti-trafficking efforts require dedicated resources, and a process as complex as collecting trafficking data is no exception. This should be considered when determining which government entity, whether a ministry or task force, has the capacity and standing to effectively galvanize a diverse set of actors on the issue. In the case of social and women's ministries, effort should be made to ensure these entities are afforded the respect they deserve, while remembering that trafficking is an issue that affects men and women alike, and thus should not be designated a "woman's issue." Lastly, adequate funding must be allocated to this issue on a sustainable basis to ensure the longevity and effectiveness of anti-trafficking policies.

- To counteract the challenge of frequent turnover in anti-trafficking task forces and directorates throughout government, AMS that do not already do so should provide better opportunities for career advancement and incentives to stay within those tracks for longer periods of time, thereby allowing people to put their specialized knowledge and training to use. This will further facilitate more robust "training of trainers" and enhance local capacity building. Combatting trafficking requires a long-term strategy and commitment. Thus, the sustainability of anti-trafficking initiatives and institutions is essential and requires the concentration and maintenance of institutional knowledge and expertise. Reliance on foreign donor-initiated training programs or NGOs cannot provide the requisite stability to combat trafficking effectively. Outside expertise must be incrementally enhanced and replaced by internal institutional capacity to effectively train new personnel and to develop and implement effective national and regional anti-trafficking strategies and measures.

- As prevalence studies are undertaken, governments should consider ways to creatively maximize existing resources. In addition to the possibility of adding questions that can gauge trafficking to national census surveys in AMS, perhaps Asian Barometer could be approached to consider the inclusion of such questions, as an example. This could be particularly illuminating in drawing connections to root causes and vulnerability factors. The survey organization, which currently operates in seven of the ten AMS, already collects data on factors such as access to public services, political participation, socioeconomic variables, and the social and economic effects of globalization.

RECOMMENDATIONS FOR THE INTERNATIONAL ANTI-TRAFFICKING COMMUNITY

- Before new global prevalence studies are undertaken, significant thought should be given to their intended purpose and design. Smaller-scale, localized prevalence studies on specific types of trafficking or designated industries should be devised based on the notion that smaller numbers do not automatically detract from the gravity of the issue, while invalid or unreliable estimates most certainly do. It would also be prudent to involve trafficking survivors more directly in the design, implementation, and analysis of surveys used to determine prevalence, leading both to better-informed methodologies and an opportunity for skill-building and survivor empowerment. In all cases, researchers, advocates, and policymakers alike must acknowledge and respect the limitations of such studies, as well as the data they are based upon. Until more reliable methods are developed, it may be best to generate estimates using multiple imperfect methods to see how widely they vary, and from there narrow in on best practices.

- To avoid wasting the efforts of ongoing trafficking data collection processes, careful thought should be given to what can be gleaned from existing databases and information-sharing resources before new endeavors are launched. More generally, both academic institutions and entities such as the Freedom Fund and newly formed Global Fund to End Modern Slavery should allocate resources for evaluating existing programs and for conducting further research on best practices in human trafficking data collection.[74] Clearly, it is best to limit the amount of funding diverted from direct services provided to trafficking survivors. But in order to ensure that more money is not wasted on ineffective programs, rigorous and independent evaluation must be undertaken on the raft of anti-trafficking programming that already has been implemented. Such research on what has been tried (and what has worked or not) will also help to limit duplicative programming efforts. Much space remains for enhanced collaboration in the anti-trafficking community to this end.

Appendices

APPENDIX 1: ETHICAL AND LEGAL CONSIDERATIONS FOR TRAFFICKING DATA

As established in the main text, the collection, storage, analysis, and dissemination of data on human trafficking requires awareness and practice of relevant ethical and legal standards. On the ethical side, working directly with survivors of trafficking will inevitably involve very personal inquiries and should focus on collecting only the most necessary information in a way that is sensitive to avoiding re/traumatization. Moreover, trafficking data will often include personal details, from names and locations of family members to socioeconomic variables to medical history. As such, it is critical to keep such data protected, particularly considering that many trafficking survivors face intimidation from their former traffickers or stigma in their home communities. Lastly, anti-trafficking NGO practitioners must be knowledgeable about relevant national privacy laws in the countries in which they operate, assuming that government entities are aware of and in compliance with relevant privacy laws.

Though in no way comprehensive, the resources highlighted below can help AMS governments and NGOs ensure their practices are in compliance with both legal and ethical standards, as well as guide ASEAN as it sets standards for regional approaches to anti-trafficking work.

World Health Organization's Ethical and Safety Recommendations for Interviewing Trafficked Women

A useful resource comes from the World Health Organization, which in 2003 published *Ethical and Safety Recommendations for Interviewing Trafficked Women* (though the guidelines are applicable to trafficked males as well). The scope of the guidelines can easily be expanded to include survivors of trafficking under the 10 basic principles of do no harm:

- know your subject and assess the risks,
- prepare referral information,
- do not make promises that you cannot fulfill,
- adequately select and prepare interpreters and co-workers,
- ensure anonymity and confidentiality,
- get informed consent,
- listen to and respect each person's assessment of their situation and risks to their safety,
- do not re-traumatize individuals,
- be prepared for emergency intervention,
- and put information collected to good use.

Specific guidelines for each of these points are available in the report online.[75]

Caring for Trafficked Persons: Guidance for Health Providers

Though targeted at health providers, guidelines published by the International Organization for Migration, the London School for Hygiene and Tropical Medicine, and the United Nations Global Initiative to Fight Trafficking in Persons (UN.GIFT) provide practical, nonclinical guidance on working with survivors of trafficking. The guidelines can help identify associated health challenges while offering approaches to providing care, including its limitations. These principles can be useful for any first responders, including law enforcement and NGO service providers. The full handbook is available online,[76] but a useful excerpt is provided below.

1. Adhere to existing recommendations in the WHO Ethical and Safety Recommendations for Interviewing Trafficked Women [see previous entry].

2. Treat all contact with trafficked persons as a potential step towards improving their health. Each encounter with a trafficked person can have positive or negative effects on their health and well-being.

3. Prioritize the safety of trafficked persons, self and staff by assessing risks and making consultative and well-informed decisions. Be aware of the safety concerns of trafficked persons and potential dangers to them or their family members.

4. Provide respectful, equitable care that does not discriminate based on gender, age, social class, religion, race or ethnicity. Health care should respect the rights and dignity of those who are vulnerable, particularly women, children, the poor and minorities.

5. Be prepared with referral information and contact details for trusted support persons for a range of assistance, including shelter, social services, counseling, legal advocacy and law enforcement. If providing information to persons who are suspected or known victims who may still be in contact with traffickers, this must be done discretely, e.g., with small pieces of paper that can be hidden.

6. Collaborate with other support services to implement prevention activities and response strategies that are cooperative and appropriate to the differing needs of trafficked persons.

7. Ensure the confidentiality and privacy of trafficked persons and their families. Put measures into place to make sure all communications with and about trafficked persons are dealt with confidentially and that each trafficked person is assured that his or her privacy will be respected.

8. Provide information in a way that each trafficked person can understand. Communicate care plans, purposes and procedures with linguistically and age-appropriate descriptions, taking the time necessary to be sure that each individual understands what is being said and has the opportunity to ask questions. This is an essential step prior to requesting informed consent.

9. Obtain voluntary, informed consent. Before sharing or transferring information about patients, and before beginning procedures to diagnose, treat or make referrals, it is necessary to obtain the patient's voluntary informed consent. If an individual agrees that information about them or others may be shared, provide only that which is necessary to

assist the individual (e.g., when making a referral to another service) or to assist others (e.g., other trafficked persons).

10. Respect the rights, choices, and dignity of each individual by:

    a. Conducting interviews in private settings.

    b. Offering the patient the option of interacting with male or female staff or interpreters. For interviews and clinical examinations of trafficked women and girls, it is of particular importance to make certain female staff and interpreters are available.

    c. Maintaining a non-judgmental and sympathetic manner and showing respect for and acceptance of each individual and his or her culture and situation.

    d. Showing patience. Do not press for information if individuals do not appear ready or willing to speak about their situation or experience.

    e. Asking only relevant questions that are necessary for the assistance being provided. Do not ask questions out of simple curiosity, e.g., about the person's virginity, money paid or earned, etc.

    f. Avoiding repeated requests for the same information through multiple interviews. When possible, ask for the individual's consent to transfer necessary information to other key service providers.

    g. Do not offer access to media, journalists or others seeking interviews with trafficked persons without their express permission. Do not coerce individuals to participate. Individuals in 'fragile' health conditions or risky circumstances should be warned against participating.

11. Avoid calling authorities, such as police or immigration services, unless given the consent of the trafficked person. Trafficked persons may have well-founded reasons to avoid authorities. Attempts should be made to discuss viable options and gain consent for actions.

12. Maintain all information about trafficked persons in secure facilities. Data and case files on trafficked persons should be coded whenever possible and kept in locked files. Electronic information should be protected by passwords.

International Privacy and Data Protection Laws

For the past few years, the global law firm DLA Piper has offered a continually expanding *Data Protection Laws of the World Handbook* on key privacy and data protection laws, as nations across the globe realize the critical importance of such regulations. Though intended as a resource for multinational corporations to understand varying legislation on privacy issues, the handbook is nonetheless a valuable resource for NGOs considering how best to protect their clients, as well as a tool for national governments to assess their laws against others in the region and beyond. Information on data protection, collection, and transfer, as well as enforcement of relevant laws, is offered for several ASEAN member states. The handbook is available online.[77]

    Similarly, the US law firm BakerHostetler compiled the *2015 International Compendium of Data Privacy Laws*, offering information on data privacy laws for dozens of countries, including Indonesia, Malaysia, the Philippines, and Singapore. The compendium is also available online.[78]

For additional information on data privacy laws in the Asian context, Graham Greenleaf's *Asian Data Privacy Laws: Trade and Human Rights Perspectives* has a wealth of knowledge on the topic generally, as well as case studies on several ASEAN nations.

European Data Protection Supervisor

Since 2004, the European Data Protection Supervisor (EDPS) has existed as an independent supervisory authority to protect personal data and privacy, and to promote best practices within European Union (EU) entities. The role comprises three pillars: monitoring EU entities' processing of personal data, advising on laws and policies that affect privacy, and coordinating with similar authorities to ensure consistent application of data protection. In 2012, EDPS provided comment on the "EU Strategy towards the Eradication of Trafficking in Human Beings 2012–2016" (available online),[79] encouraging the bloc to take data protection into account as much as possible when addressing this issue. Though a more deeply integrated regional bloc than ASEAN, the EU model is nonetheless useful as a source for coordinating regional strategy, and in its thoughtful awareness of the associated privacy concerns to anti-trafficking policies. To this aim, the EU's Agency for Fundamental Rights is currently developing a guide to assist member states in addressing rights relevant to anti-trafficking policies, with a focus on the rights of survivors. Some useful excerpts of the EDPS commentary are below, and the full text is available online.[80]

> The EDPS draws attention to the fact that addressing trafficking in human beings (THB) is an area that requires significant processing of data, in many cases involving personal data, and consequently also creates risks of intrusions into privacy. Therefore, an effective action to address THB cannot be put in place without the support of a solid data protection scheme complementing it....This is why the EDPS is convinced that the Strategy in its implementation phase would strongly benefit from inclusion of a data protection perspective and further clarification on how data protection can help this area.

> The EDPS believes that data protection should be seen as an incentive to a better implementation of the Strategy and a prerequisite to a more effective exchange of information and cooperation in this field. More importantly, data protection should not be considered as an obstacle to an effective action addressing THB. Trust is essential for victims who need to contact and rely on the authorities and other actors active in this field (such as border and asylum authorities, law-enforcement agencies, social authorities, NGOs) and also for the authorities and other institutional stakeholders themselves.

> In other words, data protection can help to promote a trust-built relationship between victims and the authorities by assuring victims—who will likely be afraid of retaliation by the traffickers—that their cases will be handled confidentially and that no information will leak out....Similarly, data protection is a key factor for trust between police and law-enforcement agencies of the Member States. Cooperation and exchange of valuable information will run more smoothly if law-enforcement agencies trust their counterparts in other Member States to only use transferred data for lawful purposes supported by strong safeguards. Similarly, compliance with applicable data protection law is important for the collection of information, as data obtained unlawfully might be inadmissible in court.

The EDPS recommends processing only anonymous data for these purposes, wherever possible. In case it is necessary to process personal data, even if they are only indirectly related to individuals, it should be ensured that the data protection and confidentiality rules are strictly respected.

Digital Security Resources

Whether due to lack of awareness or access to resources, digital data security seems to be minimally employed in the ASEAN context. As more and more information on human trafficking is stored and shared electronically in the field, the following resources may prove useful in securing that data. As governments of AMS work to enhance national and regional data collection, they will need to consider the development of data security systems that meet their unique needs.

Security in-a-Box offers guides to digital security that cover basic principles and offer step-by-step instructions for installing and using the most essential services. Resources include direct access to Internet-based tools, as well as general tactics for preventing computer viruses, securing devices, managing strong passwords, and encrypting data and communications. The resources can be accessed online.[81]

The Information Safety & Capacity Project offers a long list of links to desktop tools that can be used to protect user privacy and data integrity. The list is available online.[82]

The Electronic Privacy Information Center, an independent nonprofit research center in Washington, DC, similarly publishes a list of tools for enabling virtual private networks, email and file encryption, disk erasing, password vaults, firewalls, anti-virus software, and more. Links to relevant tools are online.[83]

APPENDIX 2: RESOURCES FOR THE IDENTIFICATION OF TRAFFICKED PERSONS

As emphasized in the text, accurate information on the prevalence of human trafficking, whether locally or globally, relies on a common understanding of the concept and robust applications for identification based on this definition. As ASEAN moves toward adopting a regional approach to address the problem, which includes understanding regional trends, it will also need to establish and implement regional standards for identifying trafficked persons. The following selections offer guidance and tools to help with this process.

International Labor Organization

In 2009, the ILO released the results of a survey—implemented in partnership with the European Commission—that focused on developing harmonized definitions and associated indicators on trafficking in human beings. Incorporating two rounds of expert consultation, the *Operational Indicators of Trafficking in Human Beings* report puts forth 67 operational indicators for both adult and child victims of trafficking. Each indicator is categorized as strong, medium, or weak. The indicators cover six dimensions that encompass the three components of the Palermo Protocol definition (an act, a means, and a purpose), and they identify various elements of deception, exploitation, abuse of vulnerability, and coercion. The report provides a matrix for evaluating a potential trafficking situation based on the presence of a combination of indicators and their strength. Though adopting this approach directly to Southeast Asia, a very different regional context, may not make sense, consideration of these indicators is nonetheless valuable. They can be useful in both training service providers and frontline responders on how to identify victims, as well as serving as a foundation upon which to design surveys aimed at assessing trafficking. The full report is available online.[84]

Building on this work, in 2012 the ILO created survey guidelines for measuring forced labor of adults and children—the *Hard to See, Harder to Count* guidelines. Knowing that common survey mechanisms fail to capture hidden populations, the ILO invested considerable resources into developing this tool, alongside national partners in 10 countries where the tool was initially tested. Such surveys have the potential to allow for the robust estimation of people in forced labor at local and national levels, as well as offer insights into root causes. In sum, the ILO sees this technique as a way of estimating the vast, hidden segment of the trafficked population.[85]

The *Hard to See, Harder to Count* tool prescribes a method for implementing such surveys. The recommended first step is to assess the relevant legal framework in which researchers will be working to set clear definitional concepts. The implementing entity is encouraged to then identify relevant stakeholders and conduct a literature review on known forms of trafficking and specific high-prevalence sectors/locales. From there, stakeholders are assembled for a workshop to review the research and establish a national—or, to extend the guidelines, a regional—set of indicators on forced labor, one which will inform the survey's scope before it is implemented. In conducting a desk review, the ILO recommends research on geographical areas where trafficking is most likely to occur; vulnerable populations; professional sectors prone to trafficking and exploitation generally, with attention to seasonal influences or perhaps even specific times of day and places of movement (border crossings, transit hubs, for example); and means of recruitment and coercion by recruiters and/or traffickers. The ILO suggests supplementing reviews of court cases, law enforcement data, and other publicly available information with key stakeholder interviews, focus groups, and direct observations. Once gathered, researchers can create a set of indicators that measures both the involuntary aspects of potential forced labor situations and the associated penalty (or menace of potential penalty) for not complying.

The ILO offers two frameworks for constructing a national set of indicators. The bottom-up approach starts by deriving a deep understanding of the local context through expert consultation, and then matching key elements with relevant indicators from the standard ILO list provided in the report. Conversely, the top-down approach reviews the standard list of indicators one by one and assesses their relevance to the local context, choosing only those that are most relevant and perhaps adapting them to the local context.

The guide further provides direction on survey design, such as consideration of where the data will be collected or how surveys can be built into an existing census. Consideration is given to some of the main strengths and weaknesses of various survey types. For example, surveying people at their place of residence is useful in gathering socioeconomic information on the household and its inhabitants. People generally feel more comfortable speaking in their homes than they might in the workplace. However, this limits the survey to populations living in "regular" households—and makes it difficult to reach those in hidden accommodations, perhaps provided by employers or traffickers, as well as those living on the street or in work camps. Targeting trafficked people or migrant workers who have returned home is a useful way to learn more about their experiences, since it will be difficult to get reliable information on household members who live or work abroad. Establishment surveys focus on people's places of work in order to collect data on the operations, employees, and supply chains. Obviously, this can be very difficult when trying to assess operations related to forced labor or human trafficking. Shadowy employers are likely to refuse access, or to intimidate workers into not participating or answering falsely. Moreover, it may be difficult to gain access to timely registries of all businesses for the purpose of random sampling. Despite the challenges, workplace surveys may help get at the demand side of the equation and allow for direct observation to look for questionable practices (assuming surveyors are properly trained in identification). Street surveys can target trafficked populations that might be working in forced prostitution or child begging, for example. This survey method uses random-walk sampling, in which a starting place and direction are randomly chosen, and subjects are interviewed at a predetermined period. Again, it might be difficult to get participants to cooperate. Likewise, border crossings are guaranteed to provide valuable information on trafficking, although surveys here would require the close participation of local authorities (which could compromise the quality of the information collected) and would be limited to brief interactions.

As for survey question design, the general elements to consider are length, clarity, reliability, wording, translation accuracy, and sensitivity to the cultural context. The guidelines provide a long list of demographic characteristics that might be relevant: household composition, including everything from gender to legal status; access to services; major events that may have affected the interviewee; employment history; economic status; and education level, among other characteristics. Indictors are established to help determine potential involuntary recruitment (e.g., third-party involvement, payment to get travel documents); life/work duress (e.g., days of leave, hazardous environments, how people are paid, how free they are to leave the home, whether they are under surveillance); and the use of coercion (e.g., debt manipulation, threats to the family, retention of identification materials).

In addition to direct population surveys, other sources of information can be considered. Service providers are a useful resource in the area of trafficking since they, alongside law enforcement, reliably come into contact with survivors. Managers or employees of shelters or vocational training centers, for example, could be interviewed about their clients. However, it would be important for a complete list of such facilities to be created and surveyed in order to maintain the statistical robustness of randomization. Surveys of media can also be useful though unlikely to be randomized or statistical in nature, thus they cannot reliably be used to determine prevalence measures, but they can reveal useful information about trafficking situations.

Whatever methods are chosen, it is important that the survey design and list of indictors are carefully tested, retested, and piloted by local interview conductors, with an eye on gender balance and adequate training in statistics and social work. All members of the research team should clearly understand the various terms and definitions employed, and careful consideration should be made to draft local translations that are accurate and contextual.

The full ILO *Hard to See, Harder to Count* report and toolkit are available online.[86]

Vera Institute—Trafficking Victim Identification Tool

Following the passage of the Trafficking Victims Protection Act in 2000, US-based Vera Institute of Justice developed a screening tool for service providers and law enforcement to better identify victims of human trafficking. The trafficking victim identification tool is intended to complement other technical training and is available in short form (16 questions) and long form (30 questions). A guide from the institute released in conjunction with the report instructs service providers and law enforcement on best practices for setting up interviews, such as ensuring that immediate needs are met and having law enforcement dress in civilian clothes, when possible, to reduce stress. The guide also offers techniques for developing trust with the interviewee, and information on confidentiality and understanding the effects of trauma (e.g., being empathetic and establishing rapport, avoiding repetition of difficult questions). Included questions center on demographics, migration information (in this case, into the United States), and working and living conditions. As this tool was developed with an eye on US trafficking legislation, it would need to be adapted to local contexts, but it does provide a thoughtful starting place. The tool, user guidelines, and technical report are available online.[87]

Transnational Referral Mechanism for Victims of Trafficking

Though not a tool for identification per se, the Transnational Referral Mechanism for Victims of Trafficking between Countries of Origin and Destination, implemented in the European Union, could be a useful reference for ASEAN as it considers a coordinated, regional approach to survivor assistance. The mechanism provides for cross-border, comprehensive assistance and/or transfer of potential or identified trafficked persons. It does that by linking the various stages of the identification and referral process— from initial screening, to formal identification and assistance, to the potential voluntary assisted return and re/integration, to legal proceedings. Obviously, it requires immense cooperation between governmental institutions, multilateral agencies, and NGOs in countries of origin, transit, and destination of the assisted survivors. These guidelines for using transnational referral mechanisms to assist countries and anti-trafficking entities in developing coordinated, comprehensive, step-by-step assistance procedures for trafficking survivors are available online.[88]

Existing ASEAN Coordination Mechanisms

As ASEAN implements the ASEAN Convention on Trafficking in Persons (ACTIP) and a related regional action plan, there are several existing instruments the body could look to for guidance and lessons learned. In 2004, ASEAN implemented the Treaty on Mutual Legal Assistance in Criminal Matters (MLAT), committing states to "render to one another the widest possible measure of mutual legal assistance in criminal matters, namely investigations, prosecutions, and resulting proceedings."[89] Since the various stages of trafficking do not always take place neatly within the borders of one nation, or among citizens of a single country, this document is highly relevant to combatting trafficking. As one of several transnational crimes of concern in the region, anti-trafficking efforts could benefit from existing bilateral and multilateral mutual assistance mechanisms, as well as from more informal cooperation between law enforcement agents in multiple countries. In providing a framework for cooperation on the investigation and prosecution of criminal cases, the MLAT should be a critical component of the regional action plan that is to accompany the forthcoming ACTIP. ASEAN's current focus on the issue of human trafficking gives occasion to resuscitate the waning MLAT, which has been employed minimally by ASEAN member states in relation to human trafficking. Though all ASEAN states have ratified the treaty, there has been very little engagement with the mechanism. Part of the problem may spring from a lack of awareness of the treaty among law enforcement personnel. In a presentation by the Indonesian National Police to the ASEAN-US Seminar on Trafficking in Persons, held in October 2014 in Yangon, the police delegation cited trafficking cases in which evidence was seized by another country, and therefore inaccessible to them. The MLAT was specifically designed to correct situations such as this.

That is not to say AMS never coordinate their efforts, as this often happens informally through direct police-to-police exchange. However, the mission of enhanced collaboration at the core of the treaty is threatened by its lack of use. Invocations of the MLAT appear to be minimal, though earlier in 2015 the treaty was used to grant a temporary reprieve to Mary Jane Veloso. A citizen of the Philippines, she faces the death penalty in Indonesia for reportedly smuggling heroin into Indonesia, though it is believed she was trafficked and forced to "mule" the drugs.[90] It is hoped that through the MLAT, Philippine investigators will gain access to evidence gathered in Indonesia that could exonerate Veloso and would help build a case against her alleged recruiters.[91]

This emphasis on inter-ASEAN coordination was supplemented in 2010 with the *ASEAN Handbook on International Legal Cooperation in Trafficking in Persons Cases*,[92] which aimed to familiarize government agencies with the use and application of cooperative legal tools relevant to trafficking offenses. In addition, the handbook sought to standardize laws, policies, and priorities among ASEAN member states, including mutual legal assistance, extradition, and securing of assets. Shortly after the handbook was published, ASEAN developed its *Specialist Anti-Trafficking Units Standard Operating Procedures for the Investigation of Trafficking in Persons Cases*. However, rigorous country-level implementation of these procedures has been slow going. The 2011 *Progress Report on Criminal Justice Responses to Trafficking in Persons in the ASEAN Region* affirmed that "unacceptably low levels of investigative quality jeopardize the whole goal of specialization."[93] It is encouraging, though, that specialist police units in Cambodia and Thailand have adopted standard operating procedures based on the ASEAN procedures, and that Indonesia developed general system-wide guidelines to help regulate the actions of law enforcement and the justice sectors on criminal cases, including those related to trafficking.

Again, the forthcoming convention and action plan provide an opportunity to ensure that such tools are further implemented for maximum impact.

Another relevant ASEAN-specific resource is ASEANstats, and more generally the bloc's "Framework of Cooperation on Statistics," established in 2001. In a 2010 plan, the head of each AMS's statistical office pledged to strengthen their mandate and capacity to better collect and disseminate regional statistics. The officials specified that they would adopt harmonized definitions, classifications, and methodologies consistent with international standards to better support regional policy planning. They further pledged to advocate to governments of AMS to invest necessary resources into more robust statistics. A strategic plan from 2011, which outlined the work to take place in the following five years, identified several challenges that remain relevant today—namely, limited resources and a weak mandate. Further attention was drawn to the overreliance on donors for discrete statistical project funding, which calls into question the process's sustainability and potential for improvement.[94] In addition, they called for proactive facilitation of technical support from the ASEAN Secretariat to sustain the data development process. It would be useful for the Working Group on Data Sharing, Analysis, Dissemination, and Communication to start a discussion on the availability of trafficking data in the region, as well as the possibilities for sharing and analysis. From there, ASEAN could consider a specific working group on trafficking data.

For the moment, ASEAN statistical resources include links to static information mostly related to the economy. However, the anti-trafficking community may be interested in the link to ILO's newly launched International Labor Migration Statistics Database for ASEAN,[95] which includes demographic and socioeconomic data on international migrant stocks and flows, as well as on nationals abroad. The actual ASEANstats database is clearly in a nascent form, but shows promise in offering both access to raw data and data in table form on international trade in goods and services, foreign direct investment, and performance on the UN's Millennium Development Goals. The latter information could be relevant to trafficking research in terms of root cause analysis by examining efforts to reduce poverty or raise education and health standards.

Lastly, though not directly related to trafficking, the ASEAN Coordinating Centre for Humanitarian Assistance on Disaster Management[96] is a worthwhile model to consider when looking toward regional coordination on trafficking. In facilitating coordination and cooperation among AMS (and with international organizations) for disaster management and emergency response, the center is a clearinghouse for consolidating and analyzing data related to disaster management. This, in turn, informs a range of activities: making policy recommendations, sharing resources and information, reviewing regional standards, coordinating research and technical activities, and facilitating joint emergency responses. It is easy to see the utility of a similar regional entity dedicated to providing similar functions on the issue of trafficking, which inflicts detrimental consequences across the region just as a natural disaster might.

APPENDIX 3: TRAFFICKING DATABASES

A database at its most basic level is simply an organized collection of information. In the context of human trafficking, a database could focus on one or more of many types of data, from biographic information on survivors and traffickers, to trafficking cases tried in domestic courts, to known trafficking routes. The benefits of collecting and storing such information in a systematic way are obvious. In the case of a regional approach to human trafficking in ASEAN, establishing a regional database will allow for standardization of the types of data that are collected—and the manner in which it is done—as well as more efficient information-sharing across relevant government entities and between governments. In an ideal world, information housed in local, national, and regional databases would be robustly collected in a standardized manner to ensure that it could be either merged or compared at a global level. Only then would we have a more accurate representation of the state of human trafficking around the world. To reiterate, a more precise understanding of the various facets of human trafficking in a given context will help ensure more effective policies can be implemented to address the problem.

Of course, simply creating a database is not a solution. Rigorous and uniform standards for data collection and entry must be followed, and resources must be continuously devoted to maintaining a comprehensive database. Though this research is focused on trafficking prevalence, the development of any human trafficking database should consider what type of information is most valuable. It must also be emphasized that any database on human trafficking will inevitably cover only the "tip of the iceberg" of observed cases. As a result, the database may show trends that are not relevant to the full scale and scope of the problem. In addition, it is unlikely that one database will be able to touch on all elements relevant to anti-trafficking efforts. It may be useful to consider multiple databases for various types of information— for example, distinct databases on victim identification and service provision, trafficking investigations and prosecutions, and information on traffickers.

Though the anti-trafficking community should celebrate the tremendous amount of attention and resources that have been devoted to this issue in the past 25 years, the proliferation of organizations and initiatives focused on the issue of human trafficking has produced some duplicative efforts. As such, before new databases or other programs aimed at information sharing are established from scratch, careful consideration should be made to ensure that they do not reproduce existing services, or at the very least are informed by best practices and lessons learned. To this end, several existing databases are highlighted here in the hopes of raising awareness about what is out there and offering guidance on how future databases might achieve compatibility. Again, this list in no way purports to be exhaustive. It only attempts to give a picture of various types of databases currently available, and to provide guidance on how ASEAN might build a regional database that is compatible with existing collections of information. Though many of these information clearinghouses could benefit from increased content, some existing resources to consider are outlined here.

International Organization for Migration (IOM) Counter-Trafficking Module

IOM's Counter-Trafficking Module (CTM) is arguably the broadest source of information on survivors of trafficking. Launched 15 years ago, the module now operates in more than 72 IOM missions worldwide as a component of the Migrant Management and Operational Systems Application (MiMOSA), and contains information on about 20,000 IOM beneficiaries.[97] The data is based on information collected from several standardized screening, intake, and processing forms used by IOM, and covers basic biographical information, details on entry into trafficking, and information on facets of exploitation. Generally, the CTM element of MiMOSA stores primary data that offers insights into the socioeconomic profiles of trafficking survivors, trafficker profiles, trafficking routes, and patterns of exploitation. However, to call CTM a database is a bit of a misnomer, as it really functions as a case management tool. That said, there is a growing awareness at the central level of the IOM that the CTM contains information valuable for researchers and policymakers in the fight against trafficking. As such, IOM's own trafficking research team is currently thinking through ways to enhance the tool's potential for informing anti-trafficking scholarship and policy. One possibility under review is to expand the available dataset by folding in partner data (if it is deemed robust and compatible) and possibly making data publicly available in a secure manner that protects the identities of the victims.

As part of this process, IOM is working toward adding more depth to the information that is collects. It is also emphasizing consistency in how the tool is used across field missions, recognizing the limitations arising from the fact that this information is sometimes collected in emergency conditions. IOM currently employs standard operating procedures to guide field staff in data collection and conducts trainings to ensure common understanding of fundamental concepts. At the same time, IOM strives to remain adaptable to the often resource-constrained realities and needs of the field offices, as explained by Harry Cook, a project officer focused on trafficking research at IOM headquarters.[98] Some of the organization's employees in the field noted the challenges of consistency in data collection and the labor-intensive process of entering data into the system. Some offices, in fact, maintain a secondary "shadow" database to collect data points not included in the standard IOM form. Also, though the IOM has guidelines to ensure that each mission is trained on database use, field office representatives indicated that these resources do not always permeate the field office culture. Likewise, local staff noted a lack of time and resources to properly implement the system's full potential. Based on the variance with which missions are collecting and processing data, a truly robust trafficking database is probably not imminent, but it is encouraging to note that the process has begun. Despite the fact that IOM's data reflects only the subset of survivors the organization has served, its uniquely broad geographical and temporal coverage suggests that existing and future databases on trafficked persons could benefit from trying to collect and catalog their information in a compatible manner.

Freedom Collaborative

Taking the aforementioned Butterfly Longitudinal Research Project as just one example of Chab Dai's work, founder Helen Sworn recognizes the uniqueness and potential value of the large amounts of data her organization is collecting year after year. "Since we are the only people doing long-term study, I feel like we have responsibility to give others access to this data in a secure, ethical manner," Sworn said. "There is no way that we as a tiny team can do this data justice."[99] This is precisely the type of data that could soon be integrated into the organization's Global Learning Community project. In that vein, Chab Dai has been operating the Freedom Collaborative, an online platform aimed at fostering collaboration across the anti-trafficking field. Since 2012, the website has offered a library, organization registry, expert profiles, and an interactive map. Through a partnership with Liberty Asia , the organization is now in the process of expanding its capabilities to potentially include an exchange for anonymized, aggregated trafficking data. Moreover, the revamped website will function more like an app than a static database—"Facebook for the anti-trafficking movement," said Sworn—complete with open and private messaging options available in any language. The platform is designed to serve diverse anti-trafficking stakeholders by creating opportunities for enhanced collaboration and information sharing, while building a supportive network for survivor service provision. The revamped website is currently in private beta, but can soon be accessed online.[100]

United Nations Office on Drugs and Crime Databases

Established in 2011, the United Nations Office on Drugs and Crime (UNODC) TIP Case Law Database[101] was developed after UNODC realized that 40 percent of countries covered in their initial global trafficking report had never recorded a single human trafficking conviction. This global database of human trafficking cases, the first such database, was created in an effort to increase the number of prosecutions and convictions of TIP crimes, while also demonstrating the effective implementation of the Palermo Protocol. The public database can be searched by country and keyword, and provides immediate access to officially documented instances of crimes—complete with details, when available, on the victims' and perpetrators' nationalities, trafficking routes, verdicts, sentencing, and other case information that can assist legal practitioners, policymakers, and researchers. The database includes information on about 1,000 cases from more than 80 countries.

Although the crimes of human trafficking and migrant smuggling are distinct, their interrelation is undeniable in Southeast Asia. What might begin as voluntary movement in search of better employment opportunities or to escape persecution can quickly transform into exploitation. As such, the Voluntary Reporting System on Migrant Smuggling and Related Conduct (VRS), launched two years ago in support of the Bali Process, may prove useful to governments and other anti-trafficking practitioners. The Internet-based secure system allows government authorities to collect and share migrant smuggling data related to scale and scope of geographical flows, major routes, fees paid, transportation and methods used, and profiles of irregular and smuggled migrants, as well as smugglers, in the hopes of identifying patterns that can inform policy. As of July 2014, the 19 participating states included five from ASEAN: Cambodia, Indonesia, Lao PDR, the Philippines, and Thailand. However, little information is available as to what extent the system is being used. Based on a list of requested data, countries could potentially be reporting a wealth of useful information. Under the principle of mutual information sharing, the VRS allows any state that inputs data into the system to access the raw data from other states. Hypothetically, ASEAN could look to this platform as a guide for launching a similar system focused broadly on human trafficking at the regional level.[102] Based on his experience developing the system, Sebastian Baumeister, an UNODC expert and analyst on migrant smuggling, cautioned that entities setting out to create a new database should remain focused on the most important types of data, and ensure that data collection is feasible in the given situation. He was confident that embedding such a mechanism into an existing regional structure—in this case, ASEAN is that "natural institution"—would help ensure its success.

Lastly, UNODC also operates the SHaring Electronic Resources and Laws On Crime (SHERLOC)[103] database, which was expanded in the past few years to include content on migrant smuggling. The database consists of several hundred summarized publications related to conceptual understanding of issues related to human trafficking, methodologies for research in the field, quantitative assessment of flows, route information, profiles of traffickers/smugglers and irregular migrants, and root cause/vulnerability factors. It is searchable by country and keyword.

Interpol

Though not accessible to the public, Interpol's numerous crime databases, accessible through the I-24/7[104] network, connect law enforcement officers in member countries for the purpose of exchanging sensitive and urgent information. Interviews indicated that law enforcement forces in AMS are aware of and using this system, though it is possible officers could engage with the resources more deeply. Authorized users may search information on suspected criminals or wanted persons, DNA profiles, and stolen or lost travel documents, among other details that could be highly pertinent to the crime of human trafficking. Furthermore, users have access to resources for standardizing the format for reporting cases of trafficking; running instant checks against Interpol's database of stolen and lost travel documents; gaining contact details for individuals responsible for people smuggling and illegal migration issues; and warning other member states if a known sex offender against minors is traveling to their territory or region.

Notes

[1]Praveen Menon and Andrew R.C. Marshall, "Malaysian Police Reveal Grim Secrets of Jungle Trafficking Camps," *Reuters*, 27 May 2015. http://www.reuters.com/article/2015/05/27/us-asia-migrants -idUSKBN0OB09E20150527.

[2] Abby Phillip, "Nearly 550 Modern-day Slaves Were Rescued from Indonesia's Fish Trade. And That's Just the Beginning," *Washington Post*, 10 April 2015. http://www.washingtonpost.com/news/morning -mix/wp/2015/04/10/nearly-550-modern-day-slaves-were-rescued-from-indonesias-fish-trade-and-that's -just-the-beginning.

[3] Emanuel Stoakes and Chris Kelly, "Asian Refugee Crisis: Trafficked Migrants Held Off Thailand in Vast 'Camp Boats,'" *Guardian*, 28 May 2015. http://www.theguardian.com/global-development /2015/may/28/asian-refugee-crisis-trafficked-migrants-held-off-thailand-camp-boats.

[4] Frank Laczko and Marco A. Gramegna, "Developing Better Indicators of Human Trafficking," *Brown Journal of World Affairs* Vol. 10, Issue 1 (2003). http://www.childtrafficking.org/pdf/user/iom _developing_better_indicators_of_human_trafficking.pdf.

[5] US Government Accountability Office, "Human Trafficking: Better Data, Strategy, and Reporting Needed to Enhance U.S. Anti-trafficking Efforts Abroad," report to the Committee on the Judiciary and the Committee on International Relations, House of Representatives, Washington, DC, July 2006.

[6] Ibid.

[7] Nicole Wallace, "Nonprofits Are Taking a Wide-Eyed Look at What Data Could Do," *Chronicle of Philanthropy*, 28 February 2014. https://philanthropy.com/article/Nonprofits-Take-a-Wide-Eyed/153547.

[8] International Labour Organization, *Hard to See, Harder to Count: Survey Guidelines to Estimate Forced Labour of Adults and Children* (Geneva: ILO, 2012). http://www.ilo.org/wcmsp5/groups/public /---ed_norm/---declaration/documents/publication/wcms_182096.pdf.

[9] Daniel Manrique-Vallier, Megan E. Price, and Anita Gohdes, "Multiple Systems Estimation Techniques for Estimating Casualties in Armed Conflicts," HRDAG Working Paper, 17 February 2012. https://hrdag.org/wp-content/uploads/2013/04/Manrique_Price_Gohdes_WorkingPaper.pdf.

[10] Bernard Silverman, "Modern Slavery: An Application of Multiple Systems Estimation," paper for the International Crime and Policing Conference 2015, prepared 27 November 2014. https://www.gov.uk /government/uploads/system/uploads/attachment_data/file/386841/Modern_Slavery_an_application_of _MSE_revised.pdf.

[11] Bryant, Katharine, Walk Free Foundation. Interviewed by Jessie Brunner, 26 May 2015.

[12] Douglas Heckathorn, "Respondent-Driven Sampling: A New Approach to the Study of Hidden Populations," *Social Problems* 44 (1997). http://www.respondentdrivensampling.org/reports/RDS1.pdf.

[13] Anne Gallager, "The Global Slavery Index Is Based on Flawed Data—Why Does No One Say So?" *Guardian*, 28 November 2014. http://www.theguardian.com/global-development/poverty- matters/2014/nov/28/global-slavery-index-walk-free-human-trafficking-anne-gallagher.

[14] Glenn Kessler, "Why You Should Be Wary of Statistics on 'Modern Slavery' and 'Trafficking,'" *Washington Post*, 24 April 2015. http://www.washingtonpost.com/blogs/fact-checker/wp/2015/04/24 /why-you-should-be-wary-of-statistics-on-modern-slavery-and-trafficking/.

[15] "Ranking the Rankings: International Comparisons Are Popular, Influential—and Sometimes Flawed," *Economist*, 8 November 2014. http://www.economist.com/news/international/21631039-international -comparisons-are-popular-influentialand-sometimes-flawed-ranking-rankings.

[16] See Walk Free Foundation's 2013 Global Slavery Index: http://www.globalslaveryindex.org/walk-free/.

[17] "Ranking the Rankings," *Economist*.

[18] Bryant, Katharine, Walk Free Foundation. Interviewed by Jessie Brunner, 26 May 2015.

[19] See Walk Free Foundation's 2014 Global Slavery Index methodology: http://d3mj66ag90b5fy.cloudfront.net/wp-content/uploads/2015/01/GSI2014_full_methodology_new -op.pdf.

[20] David, Fiona M., Walk Free Foundation. Interviewed by Jessie Brunner, 29 April 2015.

[21] Anne Gallagher, "The Global Slavery Index Is Based on Flawed Data," *Guardian*.

[22] Ibid.

[23] Ibid.

[24] "Ranking the Rankings," *Economist*.

[25] International Labour Organization. *Stopping Forced Labor*. (Geneva: ILO, September 2001). http://www.ilo.org/wcmsp5/groups/public/@dgreports/@dcomm/documents/meetingdocument /kd00014.pdf.

[26] International Labour Organization. *ILO Global Estimate of Forced Labour Results and Methodology* (Geneva: ILO, 2012). http://www.ilo.org/wcmsp5/groups/public/---ed_norm/---declaration/documents /publication/wcms_182004.pdf.

[27] Ibid.

[28] US Department of State, *2015 Trafficking in Persons Report*. http://www.state.gov/j/tip/rls/tiprpt /index.htm.

[29] Fredrickson, Terry. "Human Trafficking: Thailand Stays at Tier 3, but Hope Remains for Upgrade," *Bangkok Post*, 28 July 2015. http://www.bangkokpost.com/learning/learning-from -news/636608/human-trafficking-thailand-stays-at-tier-3-but-hope-remains-for-upgrade-next-year.

[30] US Department of State, *2013 Trafficking in Persons Report*. http://www.state.gov/j/tip/rls/tiprpt /index.htm.

[31] Annie Kelly, "How NGOs Are Using the Trafficking in Persons Report," *Guardian*, 21 June 2013. http://www.theguardian.com/global-development-professionals-network/2013/jun/21/ngos-using -trafficking-persons-report.

[32] Alison Brysk and Austin Choi-Fitzpatrick, *From Human Trafficking to Human Rights: Reframing Contemporary Slavery* (Philadelphia: University of Pennsylvania Press, 2012).

[33] Ibid.

[34] United Nations Office on Drugs and Crime, *Global Report on Trafficking in Persons* (Vienna: UNODC, 2014). https://www.unodc.org/documents/data-and-analysis/glotip/GLOTIP_2014_full_report.pdf.

[35] Fabrizio Sarrica, UNODC, interviewed by Jessie Brunner, 14 May 2015.

[36] Of relevance to ASEAN, the next Global Report on Trafficking in Persons should include further information from research conducted in Thailand.

[37] Alison Brysk and Austin Choi-Fitzpatrick, eds., *From Human Trafficking to Human Rights* (Philadelphia: University of Pennsylvania Press, 2012).

[38] Cambodian migration authorities estimated that of the 130,000 Cambodians deported in 2008, more than 100,000 came through Aranyaprathet-Poipet. Sampling for the 2009 Sentinel Surveillance study was based on these figures. The sample size calculated beforehand indicated the need to randomly sample and

interview at least 380 deportees to ensure results were representative of the full population of deportees coming through Poipet.

[39] United Nations Inter-Agency Project on Human Trafficking, *Human Trafficking Sentinel Surveillance: Poipet, Cambodia 2009–2010* (Bangkok: UNIAP, December 2010).

[40] "Risk factors for being cheated, exploited, or trafficked were determined through multivariate regression models for the entire sample of 400, which allows for multiple possible risk factors to be analyzed together to determine which are really significant, and which may interact with each other. Separating out and quantifying the effects of different variables is important because many factors related to labor migration or trafficking tend to co-vary or interact."

[41] United Nations Inter-Agency Project on Human Trafficking, *Human Trafficking Sentinel Surveillance.*

[42] Donald J. Brewster, "The Fight Against Child Sex Trafficking in Cambodia Is Far from Over," *The Washington Post*, 21 May 2015. https://www.washingtonpost.com/opinions/the-fight-against-child-sex-trafficking-in-cambodia-is-far-from-over/2015/05/21/743c8e44-ff19-11e4-805c-c3f407e5a9e9_story.html.

[43] Verité, *Forced Labor in the Production of Electronic Goods in Malaysia: A Comprehensive Study of Scope and Characteristics* (Amherst, MA: Verité, 2014). http://www.verite.org/research /electronicsmalaysia.

[44] Siobhan Miles, Heang Sophal, Lim Vanntheary, Sreang Phally, and Dane So, "The Butterfly Longitudinal Research Project: Summary of Progress Year Report 2013," Chab Dai, Phnom Penh, 2013. http://chabdai.org/download_files/Summary%20Report2013_EN.pdf.

[45] Siobhan Miles, Heang Sophal, Lim Vanntheary, Nhanh Channtha, and Sreang Phally, "Butterfly Methodology Change: A Reflection Paper," Chab Dai, Phnom Penh, 2014. http://chabdai.org /download_files/methodology_2014.pdf.

[46] International Organization for Migration, *ASEAN and Trafficking in Persons: Using Data as a Tool to Combat Trafficking in Persons* (Geneva, IOM: 2006). http://publications.iom.int/bookstore/free /ASEAN_and_trafficking_in_persons.pdf.

[47] As some of these foundational issues are addressed, it would be useful to conduct a follow-on study to the 2006 report to identify progress.

[48] Maureen McGough, "Ending Modern-Day Slavery: Using Research to Inform U.S. Anti-Human Trafficking Efforts," *National Institute of Justice Journal* No. 271 (February 2013). http://www.nij.gov /journals/271/pages/anti-human-trafficking.aspx.

[49] For example, Thailand and Cambodia do not sufficiently address the issue of "abuse of a position of vulnerability." To date, Lao PDR has not finalized anti-trafficking legislation.

[50] A secondary challenge of this lack of agreement and standardization is that survivors are often re-interviewed (thereby increasing the opportunities for potential re/traumatization) as they move through the identification process.

[51] UNIAP Office of Anti-Trafficking in Persons Committee, "Scope and Elements of Identification of Trafficked Persons." http://www.no-trafficking.org/reports_docs/legal/thailand/se_vicid_pamph_en.pdf.

[52] Patsara Jikkham, "Prayut Vows to Eliminate Human Trafficking," *Bangkok Post*, 5 June 2015. http://www.bangkokpost.com/news/politics/583721/prayut-vows-to-eliminate-human-trafficking.

[53] Royal Thai Embassy, "Thailand Will Establish Interagency Anti-Trafficking Taskforce," Thai Anti-Human Trafficking Action website, 13 July 2015. http://www.thaianti-humantraffickingaction.org /Home/?p=1499.

[54] Royal Thai Government, "Thailand's Anti-Human Trafficking Action Plan 2012–2013." http://www.nocht.m-society.go.th/album/download/b1a47ea88fdf25793b82c440b4d88f29.pdf.

[55] OSCE Office of the Special Representative and Co-ordinator for Combating Trafficking in Human Beings, *2008 Annual Report.* http://www.osce.org/cthb/36159?download=true.

[56] Transparency International, *ASEAN Integrity Community: A Vision for Transparent and Accountable Integration*, 2015. http://www.transparency.org/whatwedo/publication/asean_integrity_community.

[57] Transparency International, 2014 Corruption Perceptions Index. http://www.transparency.org/cpi.

[58] Being that this report highlights the challenges of such global indices, this index must likewise be viewed with some degree of skepticism, yet the overarching point is valid.

[59] Fabrizio Sarrica, UNODC, interviewed by Jessie Brunner, 14 May 2015.

[60] Amy Sawitta Lefevre, "Thailand Indicts 72 Human Trafficking Suspects Ahead of U.S. Report," *Reuters*, 24 July 2015. http://www.reuters.com/article/2015/07/24/us-thailand-trafficking -idUSKCN0PY0FK20150724.

[61] Steve Herman, "Malaysia Begins Exhuming Bodies from Mass Graves," *Voice of America*, 25 May 2015. http://www.voanews.com/content/malaysia-finds-suspected-migrant-graves/2789230.html.

[62] Ibid.

[63] Daniel Pye, Taing Vida, and Alice Cuddy, "Cable Shows Cartel's Reach," *Phnom Penh Post*, 12 June 2015. http://www.phnompenhpost.com/national/cable-shows-cartels-reach.

[64] Hanna Hindstrom, "In Thai Detention Centers, Female Migrants Remain in Limbo," *Al Jazeera America*, 17 June 2015. http://america.aljazeera.com/articles/2015/6/17/In-thai-detention-centers -migrants-stuck-in-limbo.html.

[65] On a related note, too heavy an emphasis on data may require IT capabilities beyond what is available. Though there may be a temptation to necessarily involve technological firms as trafficking data capabilities are explored in ASEAN states, it is important to maintain focus on long-term capabilities as to avoid the implementation of one-off projects that will lose all resources when the implementation period ends. It goes without saying that any introduction of new technology will need to come alongside substantial training on its capabilities and utility.

[66] Association of Southeast Asian Nations, "ASEAN Declaration Against Trafficking in Persons Particularly Women and Children," 29 November 2004. http://www.asean.org/communities/asean -political-security-community/item/asean-declaration-against-trafficking-in-persons-particularly-women -and-children-3.

[67] ASEAN, *Progress Report on Criminal Justice Responses to Trafficking in Persons in the ASEAN Region* (Jakarta: ASEAN, 2011). http://www.aaptip.org/2006/progress-report/Progress%20Report _Criminal%20Justice%20Responses%20to%20TIP%20in%20the%20ASEAN%20Region_2011.pdf.

[68] ASEAN, Criminal Justice Responses to Trafficking in Persons: ASEAN Practitioner Guidelines. (Vientiane: ASEAN, 2007). http://jica-cb-workshop.weebly.com/uploads/8/0/7/2/8072630/criminal _justice_responses_to_trafficking_in_persons.pdf.

[69] An ongoing baseline study on regional best practices of trafficking survivor service provisions commissioned by the ACWC will be a useful resource for building regional standards.

[70] ASEAN Parliamentarians for Human Rights, "ASEAN Parliamentarians: Horrific Discoveries in Southern Thailand Further Demonstrate the Need for Regional Action," 8 May 2015. http://www.aseanmp.org/?p=3324.

[71] "Fears Up to 6000 Southeast Asian Boat People Are Abandoned at Sea," *Guardian*, 12 May 2015. http://www.theguardian.com/world/2015/may/12/fears-up-to-6000-south-east-asian-boat-people-are -abandoned-at-sea.

[72] IOM, *ASEAN and Trafficking in Persons.*

[73] Office of the President of the Philippines: Commission on Filipinos Overseas, "Drafting of ASEAN Convention to Combat Human Trafficking Concludes in the Philippines," 22 December 2014. http://www.cfo.gov.ph/~comfil/index.php?option=com_content&view=article&id=2605:drafting-of-asean-convention-to-combat-human-trafficking-concludes-in-the-philippines&catid=108:cfo-press-release&Itemid=839.

[74] The international anti-trafficking community can eagerly await the results of a recently commissioned three-year global study on this very issue from the US Office to Monitor and Combat Trafficking in Persons.

[75] World Heath Organization, *Ethical and Safety Recommendations for Interviewing Trafficked Women* (Geneva: WHO, 2003). http://www.who.int/mip/2003/other_documents/en/Ethical_Safety-GWH.pdf.

[76] Cathy Zimmerman and Rosilyne Borland, eds. *Caring for Trafficked Persons: Guidance for Health Providers* (Geneva: IOM, 2009). http://publications.iom.int/bookstore/free/CT_Handbook.pdf.

[77] See DLA Piper's *Data Protection Laws of the World*: http://dlapiperdataprotection.com/#handbook.

[78] See BakerHostetler's *2015 International Compendium of Data Privacy Laws*: http://www.bakerlaw.com/files/Uploads/Documents/Data Breach documents/International-Compendium-of-Data-Privacy-Laws.pdf.

[79] European Commission, "The EU Strategy Towards the Eradication of Trafficking in Human Beings 2012–2016," Brussels. http://ec.europa.eu/home-affairs/doc_centre/crime/docs/trafficking_in_human_beings_eradication-2012_2016_en.pdf.

[80] European Data Protection Supervisor, "Comments on the EU Strategy Towards the Eradication of Trafficking in Human Beings 2012-2016," Brussels, 10 July 2012. https://ec.europa.eu/anti-trafficking/sites/antitrafficking/files/edps_on_the_new_eu_anti-human_trafficking_strategy_1.pdf.

[81] See Security in-a-Box website: https://securityinabox.org/en.

[82] See the ISC Project information security tools: https://iscproject.org/tools/.

[83] See the EPIC online guide to privacy tools: https://epic.org/privacy/tools.html.

[84] International Labour Organization, "Operational Indicators of Trafficking in Human Beings," March 2009. http://www.ilo.org/wcmsp5/groups/public/---ed_norm/---declaration/documents/publication/wcms_105023.pdf.

[85] At the time of the ILO's initial global estimate of forced labor in 2005, few quantitative surveys of trafficking or related crimes at the national level existed, leading them to rely on a capture-recapture technique, as described previously. This technique was repeated, though refined, in calculating the 2012 global estimate.

[86] ILO, *Hard to See, Harder to Count.* http://www.ilo.org/wcmsp5/groups/public/---ed_norm/---declaration/documents/publication/wcms_182096.pdf.

[87] See Vera Institute of Justice's tool for identifying human trafficking victims: http://www.vera.org/pubs/special/human-trafficking-identification-tool.

[88] Isabella Orfano, *Guidelines for the Development of a Transnational Referral Mechanism for Trafficked Persons in Europe* (Vienna: ICMPD, 2010). https://ec.europa.eu/anti-trafficking/sites/antitrafficking/files/icmpd_guidelines_trm-eu_2010_en_1.pdf.

[89] ASEAN, "Treaty on Mutual Legal Assistance in Criminal Matters," Kuala Lumpur, November 2004. https://www.unodc.org/tldb/pdf/Brunei_Darussalam/BRU_MLA_Treaty.pdf.

[90] Mark Merueñas, "De Lima: ASEAN Mutual Legal Assistance Treaty Saved Veloso," *GMA News*, 29 April 2015. http://www.gmanetwork.com/news/story/478474/news/nation/de-lima-asean-mutual-legal-assistance-treaty-saved-veloso.

[91] Mark Merueñas, "The Many Times the Mutual Legal Assistance Treaty Aided PHL," *GMA News,* 30 April 2015. http://www.gmanetwork.com/news/story/479246/news/specialreports/the-many-times-the-mutual-legal-assistance-treaty-aided-phl.

[92] *ASEAN Handbook on International Legal Cooperation in Trafficking in Persons Cases* (Jakarta: ASEAN Secretariat, August 2010). https://www.unodc.org/documents/human-trafficking /ASEAN_Handbook_on_International_Legal_Cooperation_in_TIP_Cases.pdf.

[93] ASEAN, *Progress Report on Criminal Justice Responses to Trafficking in Persons in the ASEAN Region* (Jakarta: ASEAN Secretariat, July 2011). http://www.aaptip.org/2006/progress-report /Progress%20Report_Criminal%20Justice%20Responses%20to%20TIP%20in%20the%20ASEAN %20Region_2011.pdf.

[94] ASEAN, *Strategic Plan for the Establishment of the ASEAN Community Statistical System (ACSS) 2011–2015* (Jakarta: ASEAN Secretariat, 5 July 2011). http://www.asean.org/images/resources/Statistics /2014/ADOPTED%20Strategic%20Plan%20FINAL-8%20July%202011R.pdf.

[95] See ASEAN labor migration statistics: http://apmigration.ilo.org/asean-labour-migration-statistics.

[96] See the AHA Centre homepage: http://www.ahacentre.org/about-aha-centre.

[97] Anvar Serojitdinov, *IOM 2011 Case Data on Human Trafficking: Global Figures and Trends* (Geneva: IOM, February 2012). http://www.humantrafficking.org/uploads/publications/IOM-Global-Trafficking -Data-on-Assisted-Cases-2012.pdf.

[98] Cook, Harry, International Organization for Migration. Interviewed by Jessie Brunner, 20 July 2015.

[99] Helen Sworn, Chab Dai, interviewed by Jessie Brunner, 29 June 2015.

[100] See Freedom Collaborative website: http://www.freedomcollaborative.org/.

[101] See the UNODC's human trafficking case law database: http://www.unodc.org/cld/index.jspx.

[102] UNODC, "Voluntary Reporting System on Migrant Smuggling and Related Conduct (VRS-MSRC)," pamphlet prepared July 2014. https://www.unodc.org/documents/southeastasiaandpacific// topics/Illicit_trafficking/migrant-smuggling/reporting_system_leaflet.pdf.

[103] See UNODC's SHERLOC database: http://www.unodc.org/cld/index-sherloc.jspx.

[104] See INTERPOL's data exchange website: http://www.interpol.int/INTERPOL-expertise/Data -exchange.

References

Anti-Trafficking Review. "Human Rights at the Border." Special Issue, No. 2, September 2013.

ASEAN Parliamentarians for Human Rights. "ASEAN Parliamentarians: Horrific Discoveries in Southern Thailand Further Demonstrate the Need for Regional Action." 8 May 2015. http://www.aseanmp.org/?p=3324.

Association of Southeast Asian Nations. "Agreement on Disaster Management and Emergency Response." Agreement signed in Vientiane, Lao PRD, 26 July 2005.

———. "ASEAN Declaration Against Trafficking in Persons Particularly Women and Children." 29 November 2004. http://www.asean.org/communities/asean-political-security-community/item/asean -declaration-against-trafficking-in-persons-particularly-women-and-children-3.

———. *ASEAN Handbook on International Legal Cooperation in Trafficking in Persons Cases.* Jakarta: ASEAN Secretariat, August 2010.

———. *ASEAN Human Rights Declaration and Phnom Penh Statement on the Adoption of the ASEAN Human Rights Declaration.* Jakarta: ASEAN Secretariat, February 2013.

———. *Progress Report on Criminal Justice Responses to Trafficking in Persons in the ASEAN Region.* Jakarta: ASEAN Secretariat, July 2011. http://www.aaptip.org/2006/progress-report/Progress%20Report _Criminal%20Justice%20Responses%20to%20TIP%20in%20the%20ASEAN%20Region_2011.pdf.

———. *Roadmap for an ASEAN Community 2009–2015.* Jakarta: ASEAN Secretariat, April 2009.

———. *Strategic Plan for the Establishment of the ASEAN Community Statistical System (ACSS) 2011– 2015.* Jakarta: ASEAN Secretariat, 5 July 2011.

———. "Treaty on Mutual Legal Assistance in Criminal Matters." Treaty signed in Kuala Lumpur, 24 November 2004.

Baker, Simon. *Migration Experiences of Cambodian Workers Deported from Thailand in 2009, 2010, and 2012: Poipet, Cambodia.* Bangkok: United Nations Action for Cooperation Against Trafficking in Persons, 2015.

———. *Migration Experiences of Lao Workers Deported from Thailand in 2013: Wang Tao, Lao PDR.* Bangkok: United Nations Action for Cooperation Against Trafficking in Persons (UN-ACT), 2015.

Belser, Patrick, Michaelle de Cock, and Farhad Mehran. "ILO Minimum Estimate of Forced Labour in the World." Geneva: International Labour Office, April 2005. http://natlex.ilo.ch/wcmsp5/groups/public/---ed _norm/---declaration/documents/publication/wcms_081913.pdf.

Berman, Jacqueline, and Phil Marshall. *Evaluation of the International Organization for Migration and Its Efforts to Combat Human Trafficking.* Oslo: Norwegian Agency for Development Cooperation, February 2011.

Biaudet, Eva. *Efforts to Combat Trafficking in Human Beings in the OSCE Area: Co-ordination and Reporting Mechanisms*. 2008 Annual Report of the OSCE Special Representative and Co-ordinator for Combating Trafficking in Human Beings Presented at the Permanent Council Meeting. Vienna: OSCE, 13 November 2008.

Brewster, Donald J. "The Fight Against Child Sex Trafficking in Cambodia Is Far from Over." *The Washington Post*, 21 May 2015. https://www.washingtonpost.com/opinions/the-fight-against-child-sex -trafficking-in-cambodia-is-far-from-over/2015/05/21/743c8e44-ff19-11e4-805c-c3f407e5a9e9 _story.html.

Brysk, Alison, and Austin Choi-Fitzpatrick. *From Human Trafficking to Human Rights: Reframing Contemporary Slavery*. Philadelphia: University of Pennsylvania Press, 2012.

Clawson, Heather J., Erin Williamson, and Ashley Garrett. "Improving Data to Combat Human Trafficking." ICF International Presidential Transition Report, Fairfax, VA, 2008.

Datta, Monti N., and Kevin Bales. "Slavery in Europe: Part 1, Estimating the Dark Figure." *Human Rights Quarterly* 35 (2013): 817–829.

David, Fiona M. *ASEAN Responses to Trafficking in Persons*. Jakarta: ASEAN Secretariat, 2006.

Economist. "Ranking the Rankings: International Comparisons Are Popular, Influential—and Sometimes Flawed." *Economist*, 8 November 2014. http://www.economist.com/news/international/21631039 -international-comparisons-are-popular-influentialand-sometimes-flawed-ranking-rankings.

Enos, Olivia. "How to Assess Human Trafficking in Asia." *Democracy and Human Rights*, Issue Brief 4403, Heritage Foundation, Washington, DC, May 2015.

Fredrickson, Terry. "Human Trafficking: Thailand Stays at Tier 3, but Hope Remains for Upgrade." *Bangkok Post*, 28 July 2015. http://www.bangkokpost.com/learning/learning-from-news/636608/human-trafficking-thailand-stays-at-tier-3-but-hope-remains-for-upgrade-next-year.

Gallagher, Anne T. "Abuse of a Position of Vulnerability and Other 'Means' Within the Definition of Trafficking in Persons." *UNODC Issue Paper*, United Nations Office on Drugs and Crime, Vienna, 2013.

———. "The Global Slavery Index Is Based on Flawed Data—Why Does No One Say So?" *Guardian*, 28 November 2014. http://www.theguardian.com/global-development/poverty-matters/2014/nov/28/global -slavery-index-walk-free-human-trafficking-anne-gallagher.

———. "The Global Slavery Index: Seduction and Obfuscation." Via the *Guardian*, November 2014. http://works.bepress.com/anne_gallagher/31.

———. "Improving the Effectiveness of the International Law of Human Trafficking: A Vision for the Future of US Trafficking in Persons Reports." *Human Rights Review* 12 (2011): 381–400.

———. "The Role of 'Consent' in the Trafficking in Persons Protocol." *UNODC Issue Paper*, United Nations Office on Drugs and Crime, Vienna, 2014.

Greenleaf, Graham. *Asian Data Privacy Laws: Trade and Human Rights Perspectives*. New York: Oxford University Press, 2014.

Guardian staff and *Associated Press*. "Fears Up to 6000 Southeast Asian Boat People Are Abandoned at Sea." *Guardian*, 12 May 2015. http://www.theguardian.com/world/2015/may/12/fears-up-to-6000-south -east-asian-boat-people-are-abandoned-at-sea.

Guth, Andrew, Robyn Anderson, Kasey Kinnard, and Hang Tran. "Proper Methodology and Methods of Collecting and Analyzing Slavery Data: An Examination of the Global Slavery Index." *Social Inclusion* 2, No. 4 (2014): 14–22.

Heckathorn, Douglas D. "Respondent-Driven Sampling: A New Approach to the Study of Hidden Populations." *Social Problems* 44, No. 2 (1997): 174–199.

Herman, Steve. "Malaysia Begins Exhuming Bodies from Mass Graves." *Voice of America*, 25 May 2015. http://www.voanews.com/content/malaysia-finds-suspected-migrant-graves/2789230.html.

Hindstrom, Hanna. "In Thai Detention Centers, Female Migrants Remain in Limbo." *Al Jazeera America*, 17 June 2015. http://america.aljazeera.com/articles/2015/6/17/In-thai-detention-centers-migrants-stuck-in -limbo.html.

International Labour Organization. *Employment Practices and Working Conditions in Thailand's Fishing Sector*. Bangkok: ILO, 2013.

———. *Hard to See, Harder to Count: Survey Guidelines to Estimate Forced Labour of Adults and Children*. Geneva: ILO, 2012. http://www.ilo.org/global/docs/WCMS_182084/lang--en/index.htm.

———. *ILO Global Estimate of Forced Labour: Results and Methodology*. Geneva: ILO, 2012. http://www.ilo.org/wcmsp5/groups/public/---ed_norm/---declaration/documents/publication /wcms_182004.pdf.

———. *Operational Indicators of Trafficking Human Beings: Results from a Delphi Survey Implemented by the ILO and the European Commission*. Geneva: ILO, September 2009.

———. *Stopping Forced Labor*. Geneva: ILO, September 2001. http://www.ilo.org/wcmsp5/groups/public/@dgreports/@dcomm/documents/meetingdocument/kd00014 .pdf.

International Organization for Migration. *ASEAN and Trafficking in Persons: Using Data as a Tool to Combat Trafficking in Persons*. Geneva: IOM, 2007. http://publications.iom.int/bookstore/free/ASEAN_and_trafficking_in_persons.pdf.

———. *IOM 2011 Case Data on Human Trafficking: Global Figures and Trends*. Geneva: IOM, February 2012.

Jikkham, Patsara. "Prayut Vows to Eliminate Human Trafficking." *Bangkok Post*, 5 June 2015. http://www.bangkokpost.com/news/politics/583721/prayut-vows-to-eliminate-human-trafficking.

Kangaspunta, Kristiina. "Mapping the Inhuman Trade: Preliminary Findings of the Database on Trafficking in Human Beings." *Forum on Crime and Society* 3, Nos. 1 and 2 (December 2003): 81–103.

Kelly, Annie. "How NGOs Are Using the Trafficking in Persons Report." *Guardian*, 21 June 2013. http://www.theguardian.com/global-development-professionals-network/2013/jun/21/ngos-using -trafficking-persons-report.

Keo, Chenda, ed. *Human Trafficking in Cambodia*. New York: Routledge, 2014.

Kessler, Glenn. "Why You Should Be Wary of Statistics on 'Modern Slavery' and 'Trafficking.'" *Washington Post*, 24 April 2015. http://www.washingtonpost.com/blogs/fact-checker/wp/2015/04/24/why -you-should-be-wary-of-statistics-on-modern-slavery-and-trafficking/.

Laczko, Frank, and Elzbieta Gozdziak, eds. *Data and Research on Human Trafficking: A Global Survey*. Geneva: International Organization for Migration, 2005.

Laczko, Frank, and Marco A. Gramegna. "Developing Better Indicators of Human Trafficking." *Brown Journal of World Affairs* 10, Issue 1 (2003). http://www.childtrafficking.org/pdf/user/iom _developing_better_indicators_of_human_trafficking.pdf.

Lefevre, Amy Sawitta. "Thailand Indicts 72 Human Trafficking Suspects Ahead of U.S. Report." *Reuters*, 24 July 2015. http://www.reuters.com/article/2015/07/24/us-thailand-trafficking -idUSKCN0PY0FK20150724.

Lewis-Beck, Michael S., Alan Bryman, and Tim Futing Liao. *The Sage Encyclopedia of Social Science Research Methods.* Thousand Oaks, CA: Sage, 2004.

Manrique-Vallier, Daniel, Megan E. Price, and Anita Gohdes. "Multiple Systems Estimation Techniques for Estimating Casualties in Armed Conflicts." HRDAG Working Paper, 17 February 2012. https://hrdag.org/wp-content/uploads/2013/04/Manrique_Price_Gohdes_WorkingPaper.pdf.

McGough, Maureen. "Ending Modern-Day Slavery: Using Research to Inform U.S. Anti-Human Trafficking Efforts." *National Institute of Justice Journal* No. 271 February 2013. http://www.nij.gov/journals/271/pages/anti-human-trafficking.aspx.

Menon, Praveen, and Andrew R.C. Marshall. "Malaysian Police Reveal Grim Secrets of Jungle Trafficking Camps." *Reuters*, 27 May 2015. http://www.reuters.com/article/2015/05/27/us-asia-migrants -idUSKBN0OB09E20150527.

Merueñas, Mark. "De Lima: ASEAN Mutual Legal Assistance Treaty Saved Veloso." *GMA News Online*, 29 April 2015. http://www.gmanetwork.com/news/story/478474/news/nation/de-lima-asean-mutual-legal -assistance-treaty-saved-veloso.

———. "The Many Times the Mutual Legal Assistance Treaty Aided PHL." *GMA News Online,* 30 April 2015. http://www.gmanetwork.com/news/story/479246/news/specialreports/the-many-times-the-mutual -legal-assistance-treaty-aided-phl.

Miles, Siobhan, Heang Sophal, Lim Vanntheary, Nhanh Channtha, and Sreang Phally. "Butterfly Methodology Change: A Reflection Paper." Butterfly Longitudinal Research Project, Chab Dai, Phnom Penh, 2014. http://chabdai.org/download_files/methodology_2014.pdf.

Miles, Siobhan, Heang Sophal, Lim Vanntheary, Sreang Phally, and Dane So. "The Butterfly Longitudinal Research Project: Summary of Progress Year Report 2013." Chab Dai, Phnom Penh, 2013. http://chabdai.org/download_files/Summary%20Report2013_EN.pdf.

Molland, Sverre. *The Perfect Business? Anti-Trafficking and the Sex Trade Along the Mekong.* Honolulu: University of Hawai'i Press, 2012.

Napier-Moore, Rebecca, ed. "Global Funding Information Sheet." *Anti-Trafficking Review* 3 (July 2014).

Office of the President of the Philippines: Commission on Filipinos Overseas. "Drafting of ASEAN Convention to Combat Human Trafficking Concludes In the Philippines," 22 December 2014. http://www.cfo.gov.ph/~comfil/index.php?option=com_content&view=article&id=2605:drafting-of -asean-convention-to-combat-human-trafficking-concludes-in-the-philippines&catid=108:cfo-press -release&Itemid=839.

Patton, Michael Quinn. *Qualitative Evaluation and Research Methods.* Newbury Park, CA: Sage Publications, 1990.

Phillip, Abby. "Nearly 550 Modern-day Slaves Were Rescued from Indonesia's Fish Trade. And That's Just the Beginning." *The Washington Post*, 10 April 2015. http://www.washingtonpost.com/news/morning-mix/wp/2015/04/10/nearly-550-modern-day-slaves-were -rescued-from-indonesias-fish-trade-and-thats-just-the-beginning/.

Pye, Daniel, Taing Vida, and Alice Cuddy. "Cable Shows Cartel's Reach." *Phnom Penh Post*, 12 June 2015. http://www.phnompenhpost.com/national/cable-shows-cartels-reach.

Royal Thai Embassy. "Thailand Will Establish Interagency Anti-Trafficking Taskforce." Thai Anti-Human Trafficking Action website, 13 July 2015. http://www.thaianti-humantraffickingaction.org/Home/?p=1499.

Royal Thai Government. "Thailand's Anti-Human Trafficking Action Plan 2012–2013." http://www.nocht.m-society.go.th/album/download/b1a47ea88fdf25793b82c440b4d88f29.pdf.

Savona, Ernesto U., and Sonia Stefanizzi, eds. *Measuring Human Trafficking: Complexities and Pitfalls*. New York: Springer, 2007.

Semaan, Salaam. "Time-Space Sampling and Respondent-Driven Sampling with Hard-to-Reach Populations." *Methodological Innovations Online* 5, No. 2 (2010): 60–75.

Silverman, Bernard. "Modern Slavery: An Application of Multiple Systems Estimation." Included in the papers of the International Crime and Policing Conference 2015, first published 29 November 2014. https://www.gov.uk/government/uploads/system/uploads/attachment_data/file/386841/Modern_Slavery_an_application_of_MSE_revised.pdf.

Steinfatt, Thomas M., and Simon Baker. *Measuring the Extent of Sex Trafficking in Cambodia: 2008*. Bangkok: United Nations Inter-Agency Project on Human Trafficking, January 2011.

Stoakes, Emanuel, and Chris Kelly. "Asian Refugee Crisis: Trafficked Migrants Held Off Thailand in Vast 'Camp Boats.'" *Guardian*, 28 May 2015. http://www.theguardian.com/global-development/2015/may/28/asian-refugee-crisis-trafficked-migrants-held-off-thailand-camp-boats.

Strategic Information Response Network. *SIREN Methodology: Statistical Methods for Estimating Numbers of Trafficking Victims*. Bangkok: United Nations Inter-Agency Project on Human Trafficking, January 2008.

Surtees, Rebecca. *Anti-Trafficking Data Collection and Information Management in the European Union—A Handbook: The Situation in the Czech Republic, Poland, Portugal, and the Slovak Republic*. Vienna: International Centre for Migration Policy Development, 2009.

Surtees, Rebecca, and Sarah Craggs. *Beneath the Surface: Methodological Issues in Research and Data Collection with Assisted Trafficking Victims*. Geneva: International Organization for Migration, 2010. http://un-act.org/publication/view/beneath-surface-methodological-issues-research-data-collection-assisted-trafficking-victims/.

Transparency International. *ASEAN Integrity Community: A Vision for Transparent and Accountable Integration*. Berlin: Transparency International, 2015. http://www.transparency.org/whatwedo/publication/asean_integrity_community.

United Nations Action for Cooperation Against Trafficking in Persons. *Annual Progress Report 2014*. Bangkok: UN-ACT, 2014. http://un-act.org/publication/view/un-act-2014-annual-report/.

United Nations Department of Economic and Social Affairs. *Designing Household Survey Samples: Practical Guidelines*. Studies in Methods, Series F. New York: United Nations, 2008.

United Nations Inter-Agency Project on Human Trafficking. *Guide to Ethics and Human Rights in Counter-Trafficking*. Bangkok: UNIAP, September 2008. http://www.no-trafficking.org/reports_docs/uniap_ethics_guidelines.pdf.

———. *Mekong Region Country Datasheets on Human Trafficking 2010*. Bangkok: UNIAP, September 2010. http://www.no-trafficking.org/reports_docs/siren/uniap_2010ht_datasheets.pdf.

———. *A Quantitative Analysis on Human Trafficking: The Case of An Giang Province*. Bangkok: UNIAP, January 2011.

———. "Scope and Elements of Identification of Trafficked Persons." Pamphlet prepared for the Office of Anti-Trafficking in Persons Committee. http://www.no-trafficking.org/reports_docs/legal/thailand/se_vicid_pamph_en.pdf.

United Nations Office on Drugs and Crime. *Final Independent Project Evaluation of Project Childhood—Protection Pillar*. Vienna: UNODC, June 2014. https://www.unodc.org/documents/evaluation/Independent_Project_Evaluations/2014/XSPT33_Independent_Project_Evaluation_Report_June_2014.pdf.

———. *Global Report on Trafficking in Persons 2014*. Vienna: UNODC, November 2014. https://www.unodc.org/documents/data-and-analysis/glotip/GLOTIP_2014_full_report.pdf.

———. *Migrant Smuggling in Asia: Current Trends and Related Challenges*. Bangkok: UNODC, April 2015.

———. *Standard Operating Procedures: SOP Manual for Law Enforcement Personnel of the Central Asia Countries on the Cases Related to Human Trafficking and Smuggling of Migrants*. Tashkent: UNODC Regional Office for Central Asia, November 2014.

———. *Toolkit to Combat Trafficking in Persons*. New York: UNODC, 2008. https://www.unodc.org/documents/human-trafficking/Toolkit-files/07-89375_Ebook%5B1%5D.pdf.

———. "Voluntary Reporting System on Migrant Smuggling and Related Conduct (VRS-MSRC): Overview of Key Questions and Reported Data." Pamphlet prepared by UNODC Vienna office, July 2014.

US Department of State. *Trafficking in Persons Report*. Washington, DC: US Department of State, 2015. http://www.state.gov/j/tip/rls/tiprpt/index.htm.

US Government Accountability Office. *Human Trafficking: Better Data, Strategy, and Reporting Needed to Enhance U.S. Anti-trafficking Efforts Abroad*. Report to the Committee on the Judiciary and Committee on International Relations, House of Representatives, Washington, DC, July 2006.

Verité. *Forced Labor in the Production of Electronic Goods in Malaysia: A Comprehensive Study of Scope and Characteristics*. Amherst, MA: Verité, 2014. http://www.verite.org/research/electronicsmalaysia.

Walk Free Foundation. *Global Slavery Index*. Australia: Walk Free Foundation, 2014. https://d3mj66ag90b5fy.cloudfront.net/wp-content/uploads/2014/11/Global_Slavery_Index_2014_final_lowres.pdf.

———. *Global Slavery Index 2014: Methodology*. Australia: Walk Free Foundation, 2014. http://d3mj66ag90b5fy.cloudfront.net/wp-content/uploads/2015/01/GSI2014_full_methodology_new-op.pdf.

———. "Using Surveys to Estimate Prevalence of Modern Slavery at a National Level: Experiences and Lessons Learnt." Australia: Walk Free Foundation, April 2015. http://asset.globalslaveryindex.org/GSI%20Surveys%20Paper_long%20version.pdf.

Wallace, Nicole. "Nonprofits Are Taking a Wide-Eyed Look at What Data Could Do." *The Chronicle of Philanthropy*, 28 February 2014. https://philanthropy.com/article/Nonprofits-Take-a-Wide Eyed/153547.

Whittaker, Matt. "State Department Clarifies Part of TIP Report Disputed by Thailand." *Undercurrent News*, 6 August 2015. http://www.undercurrentnews.com/2015/08/06/state-department-clarifies-part-of-tip-report-disputed-by-thailand/.

Wooditch, Alese. "The Efficacy of the Trafficking in Persons Report: A Review of the Evidence." *Criminal Justice Policy Review* 22, No. 4 (2011): 471–493.

World Vision International. "World Vision's End Trafficking in Persons Programme." Pamphlet prepared by World Vision East Asia Regional Office, Bangkok, 2013.

Yea, Sallie, ed. *Human Trafficking In Asia: Forcing Issues.* London: Routledge, 2014.

Zimmerman, Cathy. *WHO Ethical and Safety Recommendations for Interviewing Trafficked Women.* Geneva: World Health Organization, 2003. http://www.who.int/mip/2003/other_documents/en /Ethical_Safety-GWH.pdf.

Zimmerman, Cathy, and Rosilyne Borland, eds. *Caring for Trafficked Persons: Guidance for Health Providers.* Geneva: International Organization for Migration, 2009. http://publications.iom.int /bookstore/free/CT_Handbook.pdf.

Acknowledgments

The author would like to express gratitude to all those at the East-West Center, the WSD HANDA Center for Human Rights and International Justice at Stanford University, and the Human Rights Resource Centre for ASEAN who supported and contributed to this report. To all the sources consulted in the field and remotely, thank you for your candid insights and unwavering commitment to the critical anti-trafficking work you carry on each and every day. Special thanks go to Stephanie Fung, Vishesh Jain, and Daniel Mattes for their substantive contributions to the research. And finally, the author thanks her family and friends for their steadfast support throughout this often emotional project.

About the Author

Jessie Brunner serves as program associate at Stanford University's WSD HANDA Center for Human Rights and International Justice. In addition to student engagement and program development work, Brunner is currently undertaking research on various aspects of human trafficking in Southeast Asia and South America. She received her master's degree in International Policy Studies from Stanford University, where she focused on human rights and served as a research assistant at the Center on Democracy, Development, and the Rule of Law. Work on human rights and post-conflict reconciliation has taken Brunner to Rwanda, Argentina, Bosnia and Herzegovina, Chile, and Cambodia. In Cambodia she worked on the Asian International Justice Initiative as a trial monitor at the Extraordinary Chambers in the Courts of Cambodia. Previously, she served as a public affairs assistant at the US Department of State Bureau of Democracy, Human Rights and Labor; a reporter for the *Los Angeles Times* Community News; a non-profit public relations/marketing manager; and a freelance writer. Brunner graduated with highest distinction from UC Berkeley with a BA in Mass Communications and a Spanish minor.

About the Publishers

The **East-West Center** promotes better relations and understanding among the people and nations of the United States, Asia, and the Pacific through cooperative study, research, and dialogue. Established by the US Congress in 1960, the Center serves as a resource for information and analysis on critical issues of common concern, bringing people together to exchange views, build expertise, and develop policy options. The Center's 21-acre Honolulu campus, adjacent to the University of Hawai'i at Mānoa, is located midway between Asia and the US mainland and features research, residential, and international conference facilities. The Center's Washington, DC, office focuses on preparing the United States for an era of growing Asia Pacific prominence.

EastWestCenter.org

The **WSD HANDA Center for Human Rights and International Justice** is dedicated to promoting the rule of law, accountability, and human rights around the world, in post-conflict settings, developing countries, and in societies grappling with difficult legacies from a historical period of violent conflict. Through research and international programs, the Handa Center supports and helps improve the work of domestic courts, international tribunals, and human rights commissions around the world. Relying on a small core group of lawyers, scholars, student interns, and volunteers, the Center concentrates its resources where it can make a real difference helping people make sense of the past, come to terms with periods of violent social upheaval, and build institutions that will promote justice and accountability. The Center is further committed to increasing awareness and raising the level of discourse around new developments in the fields of human rights and international law. To this end, the Handa Center has dedicated itself to becoming a major public resource center for the study of war crimes and human rights trials, where students, scholars, and legal practitioners can take advantage of new technologies to access unique archival resources from World War II through contemporary international criminal trials.

HandaCenter.Stanford.edu

The **Asian International Justice Initiative** (AIJI) focuses on projects and partnerships related to international justice, judicial reform, the rule of law, and human rights in ASEAN and other Asia-Pacific countries. AIJI is a nearly decade-old collaboration between the East-West Center (EWC) and the WSD HANDA Center for Human Rights and International Justice at Stanford University (previously known as the Berkeley War Crimes Studies Center). AIJI combines the Asia-Pacific regional expertise of the EWC and the transitional justice research and human rights training capabilities of the Handa Center. AIJI was formed in recognition of the joint aim of the parties to foster initiatives in the Asia Pacific (or for Asia-Pacific partners) that promote standards of excellence in international justice and human rights as practiced throughout the region. Under the AIJI umbrella, the Handa Center and the EWC work in close partnership with regional and country-specific institutions to implement programs that generally promote human rights education, understanding and awareness of internationally recognized fair trial standards, and requirements for the accountability and the rule of law, especially in international criminal trials and human rights proceedings in national courts.

EastWestCenter.org/AIJI
HandaCenter.Stanford.edu

www.ingramcontent.com/pod-product-compliance
Lightning Source LLC
Chambersburg PA
CBHW051228290326

41931CB00042B/3436